erin mckenna

founder of BabyCakes NYC

bread
& butter

Gluten-Free Vegan Recipes to Fill Your Bread Basket

Photographs by Davide Luciano and Clarke Tolton

clarkson potter/publishers
new york

Published in the United States by Clarkson Potter/Publishers, an imprint
of the Crown Publishing Group, a division of Random House LLC,
a Penguin Random House Company, New York.
www.crownpublishing.com
www.clarksonpotter.com

CLARKSON POTTER is a trademark and POTTER with colophon is a registered
trademark of Random House LLC.

Library of Congress Cataloging-in-Publication Data
McKenna, Erin, 1976–
   Bread & butter / Erin McKenna ; photographs by Davide Luciano and Clarke Tolton.
      pages cm
   Includes index.
1. Gluten-free diet—Recipes. 2. Vegan cooking. 3. Baking.
I. Luciano, Davide, illustrator. II. Tolton, Clarke, illustrator.
III. BabyCakes (Bakery). IV. Title.
   RM237.86.M379 2015
   641.5'636—dc23   2014017004

ISBN 978-0-8041-3721-8
eBook ISBN 978-0-8041-3722-5

Printed in China

Book design by Ashley Tucker
Photographs by Davide Luciano appear on the following pages:
2, 10–11, 23, 24, 25, 28, 29, 33, 34, 36–37, 41, 43, 44, 47, 48,
51, 52, 55, 58–59, 61, 62, 65, 66, 69, 71, 75, 76–77, 82–83 85, 86,
88, 92, 95, 97, 98, 100, 102, 103, 104–5, 106, 107, 109,
113, 116–17, 121, 122, 123, 126, 127, 129, 131, 132,
133, 137, 138, 140–41, 142, 146, 149, 151, 152
Photographs by Clarke Tolton appear on the
following pages:
4–5, 6–7, 9, 12–13, 15, 16, 19, 26, 30, 35, 38,
56, 63, 67, 70, 72, 74, 79, 81, 87, 89, 91, 94,
111, 114–15, 119, 125, 134, 135, 143, 145, 155, 158
Jacket design by Ashley Tucker
Cover photographs: Davide Luciano (front, croissants,
and seeded rolls) and Clarke Tolton (author and cookies)

10 9 8 7 6 5 4 3 2 1

First Edition

for my daughter, halsey valentine

contents

foreword by David Lebovitz

My first visit to BabyCakes was a rendezvous with a friend who lived in New York City and raved about the place. Always up for trying a new sweet spot, I headed to the Lower East Side. Unfortunately I got hopelessly lost in that part of Manhattan, where the streets are no longer numbered but named. After exiting the subway and wandering around until I ended up at the base of the Williamsburg Bridge, I started to give up hope.

But when there's a bakery involved, I am compelled to persevere. When I finally entered the homey BabyCakes shop, I felt like I'd stepped into a little time warp. There I found counter girls in suggestively snug '50s diner garb pouring dark mugs of coffee, trays of cupcakes swirled high with frosting filling the showcases, and baked doughnuts so good they give their deep-fried counterparts a run for the money. (Now I knew how those women squeezed into those tight uniforms!) And Erin McKenna was in the kitchen, making her trademark swirl across racks and racks of bite-size cakes and confections.

As I sat at the counter with my friend, we fought over the last of the crumbs and bits of frosting left on our plates. Since that day, BabyCakes is one of my "must stop" places when I visit the city. Even though I'm not gluten-free, I love that convivial feeling I experience every time I enter the shop—including that very first time, when I instantly felt comfortable. And my badge of honor is that I've gone there so much that I've almost memorized the route. It's always a pleasure to walk in that now-familiar door and see

Erin smiling away in the bakery, presiding over her glass cases overloaded with treats.

But no man—nor woman—can live on cake alone (although I've considered trying). It's bread that is the stuff of life, and I'm thrilled that Erin has created this collection of baked goods not just for the wheat-free crowd, but for everyone who enjoys good, fresh, honest food as much as I do. Looking through the recipes, I landed on the one for homemade English Muffins (page 38) and immediately began racing around my kitchen (and making a quick trip to the nearby natural foods store), gathering up the ingredients. Because, well, what kind of person can pass up the opportunity for a warm, freshly baked English muffin with a slathering of jam? (Certainly no one I know.)

I measured and mixed, let the batter rise, and then panfried them up on the stovetop, leaning over the pan to catch that impossible-to-replicate yeasty aroma. And for once, I was actually happy to be lost—lost in the smell of frying dough. To be honest, I couldn't wait for them all to be done. As soon as the first of the English muffins were finished off in the oven, I split one open, smeared it with some homemade apricot jam, and a happy glow came over me. They were perfect.

One doesn't need to be gluten-free to appreciate breads made from the galaxy of grains that exists outside of the world of wheat. As I live a few thousand miles from Erin's bakery, I'm thrilled to be able to bake her recipes from *Bread & Butter* in my home kitchen. Which means I can take a quick trip to BabyCakes whenever I want . . . with easy-to-follow directions, too.

bread for everyone

I don't require a savory course—the dainty appetizer, some glam entrée. Because of my job as a dessertmaker, eating a meal entirely of sweets has, for better or often worse, become second nature to me. When I sit down at the dinner table, though, I find it far more difficult to pass by what comes before either of those courses, an early love that, over time and owing to a sensitivity to gluten, I had to abandon long ago: the bread basket. I admit that it is still difficult for me to live without the beautiful things inside that basket.

If you are reading this book because you have dietary restrictions of some kind, I am certain you, too, can magically weave a meal out of almost any restaurant menu—find a hidden gluten-free side dish in more polite moments, and in meaner ones add so many aggravating customizations to a main course that the chef packs up her knives and dog, moves to the woods, and closes the restaurant forever.

But there is no escaping that moment when a basket filled high with beautiful, crusty bread is presented. It brings a sudden quiet to the entire table. But instead of reaching in for a piece, we take a sip of water and watch as the others gorge themselves nonchalantly, olive oil splashing everywhere, oblivious to our suffering. We order a vodka and soda.

I need to be cautious about what I eat: I avoid gluten because I hate the intense stomachaches it gives me. (I'm lucky not to have a life-threatening reaction to it.) But no matter what one's reason might be for eliminating it from one's diet, we all *want* bread. We *want* the chewy action that gluten gives bread.

So I set out to create some vegan gluten-free recipes to fill the empty bread basket in my heart. A few early successes grew into the book you hold now. But it was very tough going from the start.

One under-caffeinated morning at the bakery, when savory bread was far from my mind as I was faced with a long baking list of desserts for the day, I forgot to add several key ingredients to a cupcake batter. It wasn't until I placed my ordinarily lovely carrot cupcakes on the rack to cool that I noticed they were dirty-blond and pocked everywhere with huge, wart-like clods.

I tasted one anyway.

The cupcakes I'd made thousands of times were now, against all odds, a pretty terrible rendition of sandwich bread—a *savory* recipe, my most feared adversary. I brewed a cup of tea and stared at these things for a long while.

Twenty-six days of refining later, the accidental savory recipe made its way onto the BabyCakes NYC menu as simple white sandwich bread. Over the next year, other breads followed.

There are reasons breads usually contain gluten-rich flours, and also reasons why nearly every gluten-free bread contains eggs (which are also never included in BabyCakes recipes). Without either, creating chewy, airy, light breads with crunchy crusts was at times an emotionally troubling undertaking. For every success there were hundreds of tear-inducing failures. But I learned something at each turn and in time I solved the Gluten-Free Vegan Bread Puzzle. I am thrilled to share the spongy, delicious, eye-opening results we have been enjoying in the BabyCakes test kitchen these past eighteen months. We hope you might profit from both our good and bad experiences.

Just remember that this is essentially a new thing we're doing together. Don't be too hard on yourself if you make a mistake here or there, and please, do not be afraid to experiment on your own. Accidents—and learning from them—are a part of vegan and gluten-free baking. Have the courage to screw up. Then laugh at your fallen dough, have a glass of wine, and hurl the dough against the wall if you like. I absolutely believe that you can taste happiness or frustration in the final product.

So smile, and fill your bread basket as high as it will go!

ingredient assistance

At the heart of what I do is a pantry full of ingredients you may not know very well (unless, of course, you have my first two books). This section covers the basics.

flours and other powders

Garbanzo–fava bean flour: I've used this bean-based blend ever since I opened the doors of BabyCakes NYC in 2005, and to this day I have not found a better, more versatile flour. Bean flour gives an extraordinary amount of lift to gluten-free baked goods, but it is critical not to over-measure as a heavy hand will absolutely result in something that tastes overwhelmingly of beans.

Bob's Red Mill Gluten-Free All-Purpose Baking Flour: Without this my kitchens would be an absolute disaster, riddled with hundreds of half-used bags left over from lame attempts to re-create what Bob's does for us already. This flour is a blend of garbanzo and fava bean flours, sorghum flour, potato starch, and arrowroot. It is a very reliable product.

Teff flour: Teff may be the tiniest grain in the world with the germ and the bran still fully intact. It is definitely among the most nutritious of flours. I find it slightly bitter when used on its own, but it adds a nice tartness to my Brown Bread recipe (page 44).

Millet flour: I cherish how light and sweet this flour is, and I turn to it to provide a tender crumb. It pairs extremely well with the more robust oat flour.

Oat flour: It is critical to read your labels and ensure that the oat flour you are purchasing is certified gluten-free, as some purveyors process wheat on the same equipment. I love whole-grain oat flour for the added fiber and because it helped me create Oat Crackies (page 122), my Wheat Thins knockoff!

Potato starch: When wheat is removed from the list of ingredients, something beyond a pinch of xanthan gum is needed to give bread elasticity. Potato starch gives recipes bounce and a subtle, tender crumb. I feel self-conscious even saying this, but I will anyway, *just to be absolutely clear*: Potato starch is not interchangeable with potato flour. You can't do it. Please don't do it.

Arrowroot: Chewiness can be elusive in gluten-free bread, but arrowroot is a welcome ally. I use it less frequently in my recipes than I do potato starch, but only because it is a bit more expensive. When you see arrowroot in my recipes, it is because the alternatives are not cutting it. As with potato starch, arrowroot is extremely potent and tends to have an overpowering flavor when too much is used. Be careful.

Xanthan gum: More than anything else, this finely ground powder adds much-needed viscosity to your cake and bread batters. It is important not to over-measure this, as it will make your baked item extremely gummy.

Chia seeds: I use chia seeds because they add a good amount of omega-3s and add a nice nutty flavor and texture. Plus the word *chia* is fun to say.

sweeteners

Vegan sugar: You'll find this ingredient at the grocery stores as evaporated cane juice, rapadura, Sucanat, turbinado sugar, and raw sugar. It comes straight from the cane and is minimally processed, unlike white sugar, which in many cases has been processed using animal bones.

Coconut sugar: I like this sugar because it is among the natural sweeteners on the market that have a low glycemic index and it is rich in potassium, magnesium, zinc, iron, and B vitamins. It is made from the sap of the coconut tree, which is dehydrated to create that granular feel we love so much. Some say it tastes like a caramelized brown sugar, and I would add that it has a hint of molasses as well. You can experiment with replacing agave nectar and vegan sugar with coconut sugar in most bread recipes.

Agave nectar: This sweetener is lower on the glycemic index than sugar and is made by extracting sap from the blue agave plant. It is sweeter than sugar, so you can use less of it. I love it for its neutral taste and for how readily available it is in most markets.

fats

Coconut oil: My preferred fat, this is full of medium-chain triglycerides that travel from your digestive tract straight to your liver, where the fat is converted for quick energy. Flavor- and texture-wise it covers perfectly for absentee butter. Buy it unscented.

Walnut oil: This very costly ingredient pops up in these pages from time to time. It is an indulgence. If you feel like giving it a try, you will find it is sweetly rich and extremely flavorful. Let's all hope it catches on so the price comes down a bit!

a guide to swapping flours

The ingredients in the following list are interchangeable measure for measure. Please, please, please do not get confused: An ingredient can ONLY be replaced with the ingredient or ingredients on the same line below.

1. **Oat flour, sorghum flour, and millet flour are interchangeable.**
2. **Teff flour and buckwheat flour are interchangeable.**
3. **Rice flour and quinoa flour are interchangeable.**
4. **Flax meal and ground chia seeds are interchangeable.**

the help desk

Welcome to the *Bread & Butter* Help Desk! Here I will answer so many of your questions in a handy question-and-answer format that I'm confident will help you bake my recipes successfully.

Q: Look, following rules isn't really my thing, so be honest: How faithful do I need to be to these recipes?
A: Great question. Answer #1: Very faithful, if you are new to these ingredients. Answer #2: Mildly faithful, if you know your way around the BabyCakes pantry, have baked at least nineteen times in your life, and are willing to make a few mistakes and lose a couple of dollars in the mistake-making process.

Q: The taste is great and all, but I'm getting these very-low-rise breads and am forced to make tiny sandwiches. That's fine, except I need to make twice as many to feed the family and I'm starting to hate sandwich day. What can I do?
A: If you add a bit more hot water (not to exceed 3 tablespoons), the dough will rise higher, but that's when things get tricky. You also need to be careful when placing the loaf in the oven so it doesn't fall. And, when rotating the bread in the oven, move extremely slowly—and the same goes for when you pull it out. The additional water makes your loaf more fragile.

Q: My bread rose really high and I was so excited, and then it shrank and shriveled up. What did I do?
A: A few things may have happened. If you added too much water in hopes of getting a higher rise, you may have gone overboard and caused your yeast to collapse from exhaustion. If you live in a humid environment, try reducing the water in the recipe by ½ cup. Another culprit is overfed yeast, a result of over-measuring your sugar. If you find your risen dough is climbing over the sides of your loaf pan, beat it down with a rubber spatula, let it rise again for 15 minutes, and get it in the oven.

Q: Can I use a rapid-rise yeast instead of active dry yeast?
A: These recipes have been developed with active dry yeast, so stick with it.

Q: Don't make fun of me, but I'm very sensitive to yeast. Is there any way around using it?
A: I'd never make fun of you out here in public because I love you! Although I haven't done proper tests, I would recommend replacing the yeast with 1 tablespoon baking powder and ¼ teaspoon baking soda if yeast is not your thing. Please note you will be sacrificing much of the taste, but desperate sensitivities call for desperate measures, as we're all aware.

Q: Can I substitute sugar for agave nectar without getting blasted in my mom circle for how terrible everything tastes?

A: Although these recipes might change slightly in texture when you swap sugar for agave nectar—or agave nectar for sugar—it won't change the final flavor too much. The rule is 2 teaspoons of agave nectar for every tablespoon of sugar listed in the measurements. You don't have to worry about altering the wet or dry ingredients since the amount used in the recipes is minimal. If you substituted sugar for agave nectar and your dough is looking too dry, just add a splash of warm water.

Q: I couldn't help myself: I cut into my bread before it was fully cooled, even though you told me not to, and it is so gummy. What gives with this rule, and can my loaf be saved?

A: Tsk, tsk. We let the bread cool to almost lukewarm before cutting into it so that the crumb has time to rest and form and finish doing its secret bread thing. Try tossing it into the freezer—now!—for 15 minutes for a rapid cool-down, but I fear you probably need to begin again.

Q: My bread tastes good, definitely, but the top is ugly and lumpy. It's a turnoff. What should I do?

A: This means your dough was a tad dehydrated. Next time add ¼ to ½ cup more water. It will loosen up the batter, help it rise, and give it a more attractive, bubble-like appearance.

Q: Do I have to make your butter for those recipes that call for it? What about chilled coconut oil instead?

A: I know it's an extra step, but the butter is essential. I tried for many months to make the recipes with chilled coconut oil, but they never came out the way I wanted.

Q: That ordinary dairy butter I'm unable to eat lasts a lifetime in the fridge. It never goes away. How long will your butter survive?

A: Mine is more temperamental, owing to the absence of preservatives, and it'll only last about two weeks in an airtight container. Unless you freeze it! Portion out in half-cup measures in silicone molds and toss them in your freezer, where the butter will last for about one month.

Q: Must I use the lecithin I noticed in the Butter recipe? I'm scared! I've never used it.

A: You must. Lecithin is essential, but don't be frightened. It binds the water and fat, creating that creamy consistency you'll need.

Q: Can I use white rice flour instead of brown rice flour?

A: No, white rice flour is too gummy. The results will be disappointing, upsetting even.

Q: I don't want to use xanthan gum or any other gum for that matter. Any tips?

A: Shauna Ahern, also known as the lovely and famous Gluten-Free Girl, has great tips on how to quit xanthan gum on her blog. It goes a bit like so (but please confirm with some research of your own): Replace the xanthan gum with a tablespoon or two of flax meal and a splash of water. But I like xanthan gum! (We've been together a long time now.)

Q: How important is it to weigh my ingredients? Is a cup measure inadequate all of a sudden? It was good enough for your other two books.
A: Controversy! This one is tough, because it creates a rift between experienced bakers and new bakers, which I absolutely hate. But I'll say it anyway: It's extremely important to weigh out these recipes. Flour can be packed, and using a cup measure will put more flour in your bowl, even if you are doing a perfectly flat measure. Wet measures, too, can often be made sloppily, and measuring them by weight ensures that you take your time and get it right. For my dessert recipes it's less important, but it becomes very obvious with these savory recipes if you're wrong. Measuring by weight gives you peace of mind. I left the cup measures in there for you daredevils.

Q: How does the bread freeze?
A: Almost perfectly using regular old plastic wrap! There are even special bread freezer bags on the market, if you want to ensure the results.

Q: Can I let my bread dough sit in the kitchen overnight? Will it become a brick?
A: You can leave it out overnight. When you wake up, punch down the dough with a rubber spatula as your oven preheats, so that the dough can rise again for at least 30 minutes. This will help make sure it doesn't fall.

Q: Tell me straight, because I'm having people over: Can I double these recipes?
A: Yes, for everything *except* the Sandwich Bread (page 47). Don't mess with that one. She is finicky.

Q: I'm dainty. Can I cut these recipes in half?
A: Yes, precious. You can halve all of them and be just fine.

The Bread Machine Question

Many of you fancies have an electronic bread-makin' machine at home. For whatever reason—and I am not making any value judgments here—I've never really taken to one. Let's just say I have a very complicated, emotional relationship with my ovens that I am careful not to disturb. Instead of betraying my loyalties, I asked for help and had my recipe super-testers give a few of these recipes a whirl in their personal bread-makers.

Their analysis: Things went very well!

A couple of amendments, though, primarily having to do with sequence. Let's use the Sandwich Bread (page 47) as an example: To bake these recipes in a bread machine, you need to first pour in the water, and then the oil and agave nectar. Then you add the flours. Only at the very end do you add the yeast. These tests were conducted at the 2-pound setting, which took about 2 hours.

So, yes, a bit different. And, granted, only a few recipes were tested, but for those we found that the ingredients and measurements worked well as is in a bread machine. Nonetheless, proceed with caution.

the waking hours

I tumble out of bed at five thirty each morning and hit the New York
City streets en route to one gym routine or another. My husband is still
very much asleep, as is—the universe willing—our daughter. By seven
I am home, where breakfast is needed.

If it weren't a little bit overboard, I'd serve pancakes every
morning until the end of time. As it stands, we limit it to once a week,
mostly because pancakes too quickly become dessert, and then what's
the point of actual dessert? Emboldened with the success of a few
early breads, I set in quickly with a few savory day-starting recipes.

English Muffins (page 38) proved to be fairly simple. Chewy, light,
and with a touch of crunch, they are cousin to the updated Biscuits
(now without spelt!) you will find on page 24. Those two braced
me mentally for tackling the elusive, mystical vegan gluten-free bagel.
I am happy to announce that I've included two types of bagels for
your family's breakfast enjoyment (see pages 26 and 28). Far more
complicated were Croissants (page 30), which relied almost
exclusively on the creation of Butter (page 133).

My hope with this chapter is to help reestablish the ability to have
a warm, if speedy, bite with your loved ones before everyone runs off
to do whatever it is everyone does nowadays.

BISCUITS vegetable home-fry biscuits PLAIN BAGELS
strawberry-lemon zest bagels CROISSANTS spelt croissants
PAIN AU CHOCOLAT socca FRENCH TOAST english muffins

biscuits

In my first book, *BabyCakes*, I offered a biscuit recipe made with spelt. Most people loved it but others cried out, "Spelt? I can't have spelt! It's wheat, kind of!" That's fair, though to reiterate, some of us wheat-sensitive people are able to tolerate spelt without issue. But no matter: This one is completely gluten-free! My suggestion is to prepare the dough before you go to bed, place it on a baking sheet, cover it with a cloth, and leave it until morning. When you wake, preheat the oven and then pop in the baking sheet. The biscuits will be done in the time it takes you to clean out the Play-Doh from your kid's teeth and strap him into the high chair!

Preheat the oven to 375°F. Line a baking sheet with parchment paper and set aside.

In a medium bowl, whisk together the brown rice flour, arrowroot, potato starch, sugar, baking powder, baking soda, yeast, xanthan gum, and salt. Add the butter and ½ cup of the cold water to the flour mixture and, using your fingertips, mix until well incorporated. Pour in the remaining ¾ cup water and mix until the dough comes together, but no more than necessary. If the dough is too dry, add more water one small splash at a time.

Dump the dough onto a lightly floured surface. Using your fingertips, press the dough out until it is about 2 inches thick. Using a 3-inch biscuit cutter, cut out biscuits and place them on the prepared baking sheet about 1 inch apart.

Bake for 12 minutes. Rotate the baking sheet 180 degrees and bake until the biscuits are baked through and the outsides are golden brown, 6 to 8 minutes. Let the biscuits cool on the baking sheet for 5 minutes before serving.

makes 8

1½ cups (210 GRAMS) brown rice flour

½ cup (60 GRAMS) arrowroot

½ cup (96 GRAMS) potato starch

2 tablespoons (28 GRAMS) vegan sugar

1 tablespoon (17 GRAMS) baking powder

1 teaspoon baking soda

2¼ teaspoons active dry yeast

1 teaspoon xanthan gum

2 teaspoons salt

¾ cup (168 GRAMS) Butter (page 133), cut into ½-inch pieces

1¼ cups (282 GRAMS) cold water

vegetable home-fry biscuits

Avert your eyes, bell-pepper haters! My husband dislikes green bell peppers so much he goes on a hunger strike if one is within fifty yards. I, on the other hand, really like them. They're crunchy and bitter and fun. But if he wants these biscuits, I either leave the green peppers out or swap in something else, like a leek or some celery. The point I'm trying to make is this: You can substitute things in this recipe, as long as they are similar in texture! Don't put a mushroom in: It will absorb all the moisture. But a jalapeño instead of a green pepper? That could be fantastic!

1 recipe dough for Biscuits (opposite)

½ red bell pepper, chopped

½ green bell pepper, chopped

½ small yellow onion, chopped

¼ teaspoon paprika

½ teaspoon salt

Freshly ground black pepper

2 tablespoons (28 GRAMS) melted unscented coconut oil

Leaves from 1 sprig rosemary

Preheat the oven to 375°F. Line a baking sheet with parchment paper and set aside.

Prepare the biscuit dough.

In a medium bowl, combine the red and green bell pepper, onion, paprika, salt, and a little black pepper. Add the oil and rosemary and toss together. Using a rubber spatula, fold the vegetables into the biscuit dough.

Dump the dough onto a lightly floured work surface. Using your fingertips, press the dough out until it is about 2 inches high. Using a 3-inch biscuit cutter, cut out biscuits and put them on the prepared sheet about 1 inch apart.

Bake for 12 minutes. Rotate the sheet 180 degrees and bake until the biscuits are baked through and the outsides are golden brown, 6 to 8 minutes. Let the biscuits cool on the baking sheet for 5 minutes before serving.

plain bagels

Re-creating the unique texture and flavor of the classic New York City bagel in a vegan and gluten-free iteration had me sobbing fitful tears. I traveled around New York City like a possessed person, eager to taste-test others' nontraditional bagels, only to discover what I always discover: Gluten-free is one thing, and vegan and gluten-free is something else entirely. Without eggs, gluten-free bagels are typically extremely dense. But obviously using eggs was a nonstarter. So I used my trusted formula of adding a bit more arrowroot and a dose of hot water and found slight success. I eventually learned that it was the centuries-old boil-and-bake technique foiling my recipe—I'd need to forgo boiling. Ultimately, the trusty BabyCakes kitchen staff convinced me that the simple, even lazy technique that follows is by far the best method given the ingredients.

makes 12

¼ cup (33 GRAMS) **cornmeal, for the baking sheet**

2 cups minus 1 teaspoon (198 GRAMS) **gluten-free oat flour**

1 cup (140 GRAMS) **brown rice flour**

1 cup (120 GRAMS) **arrowroot**

¾ cup (144 GRAMS) **potato starch**

⅓ cup (70 GRAMS) **vegan sugar**

2¼ teaspoons **active dry yeast**

1 tablespoon (15 GRAMS) **baking powder**

¼ teaspoon **baking soda**

1 teaspoon **xanthan gum**

1 teaspoon **salt**

1¾ cups (395 GRAMS) **warm rice milk (about 100°F)**

⅓ cup (70 GRAMS) **coconut milk**

⅓ cup (70 GRAMS) **melted unscented coconut oil, plus more for brushing**

Line 2 baking sheets with parchment paper, sprinkle generously with the cornmeal, and set aside.

In a medium bowl, whisk together the flours, arrowroot, potato starch, sugar, yeast, baking powder, baking soda, xanthan gum, and salt. Pour in the warm rice milk, coconut milk, and coconut oil and, using a rubber spatula, stir until a sticky dough forms. Place the dough in the refrigerator and let it chill for 1 hour, until firm.

Remove the dough from the refrigerator and, using a large ice cream scoop, measure out 12 heaping portions onto the prepared baking sheets 2½ inches apart and roll into balls. Wet your fingertips and form a hole in the center of each ball of dough to create the shape of a bagel. Cover the dough with a dish towel and let it sit on the countertop for 1 hour.

Preheat the oven to 400°F.

Uncover the bagels and bake them for 10 minutes. Brush them with a little coconut oil, rotate the baking sheet 180 degrees, and bake until golden brown, 6 minutes. Let the bagels cool on the baking sheet for 10 minutes before serving.

I am always thinking of sweets, which made writing this book particularly tricky. I'd say constantly, "Stay on track, Erin. Focus. Finish this brownie and get back to work." But soon enough I'd be staring off into space and eating a cookie in frustration. Eventually I'd find an ingredient that curbed those cravings and allowed me to proceed. This is one of those recipes, and the ingredient is lemon zest. Strawberries and lemon zest locked inside a bagel deliver a bitter-yet-tangy solution that is both savory and sweet. I'm especially proud of this one, because it really stretches my creativity.

Line 2 baking sheets with parchment paper, sprinkle generously with the cornmeal, and set aside.

In a medium bowl, whisk together the flours, arrowroot, potato starch, sugar, yeast, baking powder, baking soda, xanthan gum, and salt. Pour in the milks, coconut oil, and lemon extract and, using a rubber spatula, stir until a sticky dough forms. Gently fold in the strawberries and lemon zest. Place the dough in the refrigerator and let it chill for 1 hour, until firm.

Remove the dough from the refrigerator and, using a large ice cream scoop, measure out 14 heaping portions onto the prepared baking sheets 2½ inches apart and roll into balls. Wet your fingertips and form a hole in the center of each ball of dough to create the shape of a bagel. Cover the dough with a dish towel and let it sit on the countertop for 1 hour.

Preheat the oven to 400°F.

Uncover the bagels and bake for 10 minutes. Brush the bagels with a little coconut oil, rotate the baking sheet 180 degrees, and bake until golden brown, 6 minutes. Let the bagels cool on the baking sheet for 5 minutes before serving.

makes 14

¼ cup (33 GRAMS) cornmeal, for the baking sheet

2 cups (200 GRAMS) gluten-free oat flour

1 cup (140 GRAMS) brown rice flour

1 cup (120 GRAMS) arrowroot

¾ cup (144 GRAMS) potato starch

⅓ cup (70 GRAMS) vegan sugar

2¼ teaspoons active dry yeast

1 tablespoon (15 GRAMS) baking powder

¼ teaspoon baking soda

1 teaspoon xanthan gum

1 teaspoon salt

1½ cups (339 GRAMS) rice milk

⅓ cup (70 GRAMS) coconut milk

⅓ cup (70 GRAMS) melted unscented coconut oil, plus more for brushing

1 teaspoon lemon extract

1 cup (152 GRAMS) strawberries, sliced

1 tablespoon (2 GRAMS) grated lemon zest

strawberry–lemon zest bagels

croissants

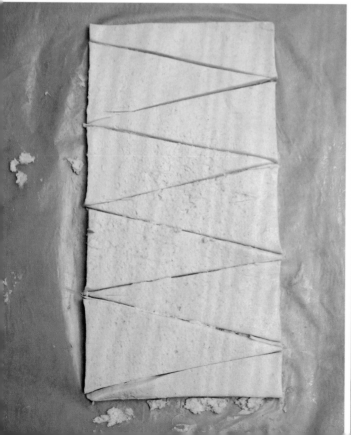

Some of you may remember that very trippy era when sandwiches were served on croissants instead of bread and with sprouts instead of lettuce. It was the eighties, and the days were ripe with sun-dried tomatoes and the early lessons of California cuisine, which taught me that I dislike sprouts and sun-dried tomatoes. For that reason, I keep my croissants confined to the breakfast table. But of course you can do whatever you'd like with this recipe! Follow the instructions carefully on your way to flaky, buttery, sweetly salted bliss. Oui, I say! Oui!

1¼ cups (125 GRAMS) gluten-free oat flour

1 cup plus 1 teaspoon (123 GRAMS) arrowroot, plus more for dusting

¾ cup (144 GRAMS) potato starch

2¼ teaspoons active dry yeast

2 tablespoons (28 GRAMS) vegan sugar

2 teaspoons salt

1 teaspoon baking powder

1 teaspoon xanthan gum

¾ cup (169 GRAMS) room-temperature rice milk

½ cup (113 GRAMS) room-temperature coconut milk

1 cup (224 GRAMS) Butter (page 133), chilled

¼ cup (56 GRAMS) melted unscented coconut oil

In a medium bowl, whisk together the flour, arrowroot, potato starch, yeast, sugar, salt, baking powder, and xanthan gum. Pour in the milks and continue to whisk until the dough is silky and pulls away from the sides of the bowl easily. Add more arrowroot 1 tablespoon at a time if the batter is too wet. Wrap the dough in plastic wrap and refrigerate for 2 hours.

Transfer the chilled dough to a food processor and crumble in the butter in large pieces with your hands. Pulse the dough until it is dotted with quarter-size pieces of butter. Wrap the dough in plastic wrap and refrigerate for 1 hour.

Line a baking sheet with parchment paper and set aside.

Remove the dough from the refrigerator, unwrap it, and cut it in half. Between 2 sheets of parchment paper, roll out each portion into a rectangle that is about 18 by 6 inches. Trim off the rough edges of the dough to create 2 clean rectangles. Remove the parchment paper and, using a knife, cut the dough into 6-inch rectangles. Cut the squares diagonally to make triangles. Roll the two widest points toward the top of the triangle and curve the dough to create a crescent shape. Place the croissants on the reserved baking sheet, brush with coconut oil, cover with a dish towel, and let rise for 1 hour.

Preheat the oven to 375°F.

Bake the croissants for 12 minutes. Rotate the baking sheet 180 degrees and bake until golden brown, 6 minutes. Let cool on the sheet for 10 minutes before serving.

spelt croissants

This recipe is not a major departure from its gluten-free sister on page 30, but like every sibling, it has its own uniquely contrarian personality. For the uninitiated, spelt is a distant relative of wheat that doesn't share some of wheat's debilitating characteristics. Some people with wheat sensitivities can digest it without incident.

Make the butter square: Remove the butter from the refrigerator and let it soften for 15 minutes.

In a medium bowl, combine the butter and the flour and work them together with your hands. Loosely wrap the butter mixture in plastic wrap and press it into a 7-inch square. Refrigerate for 1 hour.

Make the croissant dough: In a medium bowl, whisk together the flour, sugar, yeast, salt, and baking powder. Pour in the rice milk and coconut oil and, using a rubber spatula, stir until a sticky dough forms. Wrap the dough in plastic wrap and refrigerate for 1 hour.

Remove the dough and the butter square from the refrigerator and unwrap it. Between 2 sheets of parchment paper, roll the dough out into an 11-inch square. Remove the top sheet of parchment. Put the butter square diagonally on top of the dough. Fold the corners of the dough over the butter square and seal the edges together. Starting at the edge nearest you, using a rolling pin, press down and forward on the dough every inch so the butter square spreads evenly inside. Roll the dough out into a 14-inch square. Fold the dough over in thirds vertically, like a business letter,

makes 12

BUTTER SQUARE

1¼ cups (280 GRAMS) Butter (page 133)

2 tablespoons (18 GRAMS) white spelt flour

CROISSANT DOUGH

3 cups (420 GRAMS) white spelt flour

¼ cup (56 GRAMS) vegan sugar

2¼ teaspoons active dry yeast

2 teaspoons salt

1 teaspoon baking powder

1⅓ cups (300 GRAMS) room-temperature rice milk

2 tablespoons (28 GRAMS) melted unscented coconut oil, plus more for brushing

and then fold it in thirds horizontal to create a thick square. Wrap the dough in plastic wrap and refrigerate for 1 hour.

Remove the dough from the refrigerator and repeat the process above. Refrigerate for 1 more hour.

Line 2 baking sheets with parchment paper and set aside.

Remove the dough from the refrigerator, unwrap it, and cut it in half. Between 2 sheets of parchment paper, roll out each portion into a rectangle that's about 18 inches by 6 inches. Remove the parchment paper and trim off the rough edges of the dough to create 2 clean rectangles. Cut the dough into 6-inch rectangles, and cut the squares diagonally to make triangles. Roll the two widest points toward the top of the triangle and curve the dough to create a crescent shape. Place the croissants on the prepared baking sheets. Brush the croissants with oil, cover with a dish towel, and let rise for 1 hour.

Preheat the oven to 375°F.

Bake the croissants for 12 minutes, and rotate the baking sheets 180 degrees. Bake until they are golden brown, 6 minutes. Let the croissants cool on the baking sheets for 10 minutes before serving.

pain au chocolat

My seven-year-old nephew and longtime BabyCakes super-representative, Oliver, is among the world's fussiest eaters. Two things he'll never pass over are the chocolate chip cookies from my first book and chocolate croissants. "I like the chocolate with the soft bread on top of it," he explained when asked about his love of pain au chocolat. A quick note: Now is not the time to use cheap chocolate—not that it ever is, but especially not now. Trust me. I use Enjoy Life brand chocolate chips.

makes 14

¼ cup (56 GRAMS) melted unscented coconut oil

2 tablespoons (44 GRAMS) agave nectar

1 recipe dough for Croissants (page 30) or Spelt Croissants (page 32)

1 cup (160 GRAMS) semisweet vegan chocolate chips

⅓ cup (70 GRAMS) vegan sugar

Line 2 baking sheets with parchment paper. In a small cup, combine the coconut oil and agave nectar and set aside.

Prepare the dough and refrigerate it for 1 hour.

Remove the dough from the refrigerator, put it between 2 pieces of parchment paper, and roll it out into a 10 by 18-inch rectangle. Remove the parchment paper and cut the dough into 6-inch rectangles. Put the rectangles on the prepared baking sheets, with the long ends facing you. Sprinkle 2 teaspoons of the chocolate chips vertically down the middle of each rectangle. Fold the right edge of the dough over the chocolate chips and seal about two thirds of the way from the left side. Sprinkle 2 more teaspoons of the chocolate chips along the seam of the folded dough. Fold the left edge of the dough over just beyond dead center and pinch the dough to seal. Flip the dough so the seam side is down. Cover the croissants with a dish towel and let rise for 1 hour.

Preheat the oven to 375°F.

Brush the pain au chocolat with the oil mixture and sprinkle with sugar. Bake for 12 minutes, and rotate the baking sheets 180 degrees. Bake until they are golden brown, 6 minutes more. Let the pain au chocolat cool on the baking sheets for 10 minutes before serving.

socca

I learned of this beautiful, deliciously exotic (to me anyway!) recipe from my great friend David Lebovitz, the indomitable author of *The Sweet Life in Paris*, *Ready for Dessert*, this book's foreword, and many other gorgeously written things. As an American expat living in Paris, France, David explained to me that *socca* is a savory, crepe-like recipe that the French make using chickpea flour—a naturally gluten-free recipe that I obviously needed to Erin-size! Abroad, these are made a bit thinner than I prefer; if you like them even more substantial, cut the rice milk in half and you'll be set. Top a socca with some caramelized onions, sautéed kale, or roasted vegetables and you've got a perfectly delicious and rewarding lunch.

makes 8

1 cup (92 GRAMS) chickpea flour

2 tablespoons (28 GRAMS) vegan sugar

¼ teaspoon xanthan gum

¼ teaspoon paprika

¼ teaspoon baking powder

2 teaspoons salt

1 cup (226 GRAMS) rice milk

1 garlic clove, minced

Olive oil, for the skillet

Place 2 paper towels on a large plate and set aside.

In a medium bowl, whisk together the chickpea flour, sugar, xanthan gum, paprika, baking powder, and salt. Pour in the rice milk, add the garlic, and stir until a pancake-like batter forms.

Heat 1 teaspoon of oil in a wide skillet set over medium-high heat. Using a ¼-cup measure, pour the batter into the skillet (there should be room to cook 2 at a time) and tilt the pan slightly so that the batter spreads. Cook until the bottoms are browned and the top is bubbling, 2 to 3 minutes. Flip and cook until the second side has browned, 2 minutes. Transfer the socca to the prepared plate. Repeat the process with the remaining batter.

Serve immediately.

french toast

I fell down the research rabbit-hole when learning about French toast. The gist: The dish dates back to about the fourth or fifth *century* (!), it has since been re-created in one form or another by all the big bread-eating cultures, and you can really do anything you want to it. No rules. Mine is savory, because you can always add sweetness but it's tough to remove it.

In a small bowl, whisk together the oat flour, arrowroot, cinnamon (if using), and salt. Pour in the rice milk and agave nectar and whisk until smooth.

In a sauté pan set over medium heat, melt the butter. Dunk a slice of bread in the milk mixture, coating both sides. Put the bread on the pan and cook until browned and crisp, 2 minutes. Flip it over and cook until the second side is brown and crisp, about 2 minutes. Transfer to a serving plate and repeat the process with the remaining ingredients. Serve immediately with butter.

serves 6

½ cup (50 GRAMS) gluten-free oat flour

2 tablespoons (15 GRAMS) arrowroot

1 teaspoon ground cinnamon (optional)

½ teaspoon salt

¾ cup (169 GRAMS) rice milk

1 tablespoon (22 GRAMS) agave nectar

1 tablespoon (14 GRAMS) Butter (page 133), plus more for serving

6 (1-inch-thick) slices day-old Sandwich Bread (page 47)

french toast four ways

Crunchy French Toast: Take a heaping handful of the gluten-free cereal of your choosing and smash it with . . . something. Let your kid do it. After you've dunked your bread in the French toast batter, roll it in the cereal crumbs before tossing it into the sauté pan and cooking as you would regular old French toast. Keep an eye on it as it cooks! I find that giving your pan a bit of a shake here and there prevents singed spots.

Baked French Toast with Fruit Compote: Make a quick compote by simmering your favorite berries or stone fruit in a saucepan with a few tablespoons of sugar or agave nectar over medium heat until the fruit becomes soft. Place the prepared French toast on a baking sheet, top with the fruit, and bake at 350°F until brown and crisp, about 20 minutes. Top with vegan powdered sugar and serve.

Cinnamon-Sugar French Toast Rolls: Once the French toast is cooked, spread a teaspoon of Butter (page 133) on top, sprinkle with however much cinnamon and sugar you prefer, and roll it up like a jelly roll. Growing up, my sisters and I were convinced it tasted better like this, and I've yet to uncover evidence proving us wrong.

Maple French Toast, Hold the Syrup: To get the same flavor of maple-drenched French toast without the extra sugar, add 1 teaspoon maple flavoring to the French toast batter and proceed with the recipe.

english muffins

The English muffin–eating techniques you learned from the beloved Thomas' brand during childhood apply to my knockoff: Split them with a fork, pull the sides apart gently while monitoring that they are proportioned equally, and spread on that Butter (page 133) quickly so it seeps deep inside those "nooks" and "crannies." Or make a pizza out of them if you want! You can also dust the top and bottom with coarse cornmeal before baking so your children can authentically make a mess of your table and floor with crunchy enjoyment.

In a small bowl, stir together the warm rice milk, sugar, and yeast. Let sit until it bubbles, about 10 minutes.

In a medium bowl, whisk together the potato starch, flours, xanthan gum, salt, and baking soda. Pour in the yeast mixture, oil, and apple cider vinegar and, using a rubber spatula, stir until a batter-like dough forms. If the dough is too dry, add additional warm rice milk, 2 tablespoons at a time, until it loosens up. Cover the dough with a dish towel and let it sit on the countertop for 1 hour.

Preheat the oven to 350°F. Line a baking sheet with parchment paper and set aside.

Heat 1 teaspoon of the oil in a wide skillet set over medium heat. Brush the insides of 4 (3-inch) muffin rings with oil and put them inside the skillet. Sprinkle the bottom of each ring with cornmeal and fill each two-thirds high with batter. Cook for 3½ minutes or until browned. Flip the muffins and cook until the second side has browned, about 2 more minutes. Transfer the muffins to the reserved baking sheet. Carefully run a butter knife around the sides of each muffin and remove the ring. Repeat this process with the remaining batter. Once all the muffins are browned and arranged on the baking sheet, bake until cooked through, 8 to 10 minutes. Let the muffins cool on the baking sheet for 10 minutes before serving.

makes 5

2 cups (452 GRAMS) **warm rice milk (about 100 to 110°F), plus more as needed**

2 tablespoons plus 1 teaspoon (32 GRAMS) **vegan sugar**

2¼ teaspoons active dry yeast

1 cup (192 GRAMS) **potato starch**

1 cup (100 GRAMS) **gluten-free oat flour**

½ cup (70 GRAMS) **brown rice flour**

1½ teaspoons xanthan gum

1 teaspoon salt

1 teaspoon baking soda

4 tablespoons (56 GRAMS) **melted unscented coconut oil, plus more for the skillet**

1 teaspoon apple cider vinegar

¼ cup (33 GRAMS) **cornmeal**

breads

Here we go! Savory breads are the Mount Everest of vegan and gluten-free baking. They are the intimidating peak that sends brave bakers home shell-shocked, with crushed dreams and battered egos. Unlike with desserts, there's no relying on frosting for cover. I didn't even try to make a savory bread for my first eight years as a baker. I admit I was afraid. Eventually I locked myself in the kitchen and did battle.

When I emerged a year or so later, bruised and bewildered and with burns up and down my arms, I wore a large smile and bore many of the recipes found in the following pages.

Before we begin, though, let's do some of the background stuff. Gluten, as you probably know by now, is the thing that gives bread its unmistakable *bread-ness*: the spongy, airy, and chewy texture. Without it, baking—and baking bread in particular—is extremely difficult. But in some ways I find this fact liberating. As a rule, I seriously hate rules. But if we were to remove bread's most fundamental ingredient (gluten), and also its off-limits conspirator (egg), well, that just about entirely opens the field. I hope you find this exciting like I do. (Perhaps you are slightly less masochistic.)

rye bread CINNAMON-RAISIN BREAD brown bread
PUMPERNICKEL BREAD sandwich bread SALTY-SWEET SESAME BREAD
wrap bread FLAX MEAL BREAD spicy vegetable cornbread
CARROT BREAD sweet potato and sage pull-apart rolls SEEDED ROLLS

rye bread

For many years I confused this bread as being strictly for grandfathers who eat it toasted and dry with black coffee while reading the newspaper and looking grouchy. Then I moved to New York and thought of it as belonging exclusively to the pastrami sandwich. Now, having actually tasted it, I think it is for everything, on every occasion.

Lightly grease a 7 by 4 by 3-inch loaf pan with oil.

In a small bowl, combine the coconut oil, warm water, agave nectar, and yeast. Stir once and set aside until it bubbles, about 10 minutes.

In a large bowl, whisk together the flours, potato starch, arrowroot, baking powder, xanthan gum, caraway seeds, and salt. Add the yeast mixture and, using a rubber spatula, stir until it is the consistency of cake batter. If the dough is too thick, add additional warm water one splash at a time. Pour the batter into the prepared loaf pan, cover with a dish towel, and let the dough rise for 1 hour.

Preheat the oven to 400°F.

Bake the bread for 20 minutes, and then rotate the pan 180 degrees. Bake until the crust is golden and a toothpick inserted in the center comes out clean, about 15 minutes. Let the bread cool in the pan for 1 hour before slicing.

makes one 7 by 4 by 3-inch loaf

- 2 teaspoons melted unscented coconut oil, plus more for the pan
- 2¼ cups (508 GRAMS) warm water (about 100°F)
- 2 tablespoons (44 GRAMS) agave nectar
- 2¼ teaspoons active dry yeast
- 1 cup (100 GRAMS) gluten-free oat flour
- ½ cup (60 GRAMS) millet flour
- ¼ cup (30 GRAMS) teff flour
- ¾ cup (144 GRAMS) potato starch
- ½ cup (60 GRAMS) arrowroot
- 1 teaspoon baking powder
- 1½ teaspoons xanthan gum
- 2 tablespoons (16 GRAMS) caraway seeds
- 1½ teaspoons salt

cinnamon-raisin bread

I am on the record as one who dislikes cooked raisins. A fake poll reveals that I represent 41 percent of the population. My dad loves them, for example. But even I can admit that there are combinations that cannot be denied. This is one of them.

Lightly grease a 7 by 4 by 3-inch loaf pan with oil.

In a small bowl, combine the warm rice milk, agave nectar, and yeast. Stir once and set aside to proof until it bubbles, about 10 minutes.

In a medium bowl, whisk together the flours, arrowroot, potato starch, sugar, salt, baking powder, xanthan gum, cinnamon, and raisins. Pour in the oil and the yeast mixture and, using a rubber spatula, stir until it is the consistency of cake batter. If the dough is too thick, add warm water one splash at a time. Pour the dough into the prepared loaf pan, cover with a dish towel, and let the dough rise for 1 hour.

Preheat the oven to 400°F.

Bake the bread for 20 minutes, and then rotate the pan 180 degrees. Bake until the crust is golden and a toothpick inserted in the center comes out clean, about 15 minutes.

Let the bread cool in the pan for 1 hour before slicing.

makes one 7 by 4 by 3-inch loaf

- 2 teaspoons (9 GRAMS) melted unscented coconut oil, plus more for the pan
- 2¼ cups (508 GRAMS) warm rice milk (about 100°F)
- 2 tablespoons (44 GRAMS) agave nectar
- 2¼ teaspoons active dry yeast
- 1 cup (100 GRAMS) gluten-free oat flour
- ¾ cup plus 1 tablespoon (114 GRAMS) brown rice flour
- ½ cup (60 GRAMS) arrowroot
- 1 cup (192 GRAMS) potato starch
- 2 tablespoons (28 GRAMS) vegan sugar
- 2 teaspoons salt
- 1 teaspoon baking powder
- ½ teaspoon xanthan gum
- 2 teaspoons ground cinnamon
- ⅔ cup (84 GRAMS) raisins

brown bread

This will be easily mistaken for wheat bread. In fact, it so closely mimics a wheat bread that if you made it for an unsuspecting gluten-free friend who has never had it before, she or he would think twice before trying a slice for fear of all the presumed wheat. It remains one of my absolute favorite breads, but even in its splendor I still can't make any sense of how it works exactly. That makes me love it even more.

Lightly grease a 7 by 4 by 3-inch loaf pan with oil.

In a small bowl, combine the warm water, sugar, and yeast. Stir once and set aside to proof until it bubbles, about 10 minutes. Add the 1 tablespoon melted coconut oil and give it a stir.

In a medium bowl, whisk together the ground flaxseed, flours, potato starch, arrowroot, cocoa powder, xanthan gum, baking powder, and salt. Pour in the yeast mixture and, using a rubber spatula, stir until it is the consistency of cake batter. If the dough is too thick, add additional warm water one splash at a time. Pour the dough into the prepared loaf pan, cover with a dish towel, and let the dough rise for 1 hour.

Preheat the oven to 400°F.

Bake the bread for 20 minutes, and then rotate the pan 180 degrees. Bake until the crust is golden brown and a toothpick inserted in the center comes out clean, about 15 minutes. Let the bread cool in the pan for 1 hour before slicing.

makes one 7 by 4 by 3-inch loaf

- 1 tablespoon (14 GRAMS) melted unscented coconut oil, plus more for the pan
- 1½ cups (339 GRAMS) warm water (about 100°F)
- 3 tablespoons (42 GRAMS) vegan sugar
- 2¼ teaspoons active dry yeast
- ⅓ cup (35 GRAMS) ground flaxseed (flax meal)
- 2⅔ cups (266 GRAMS) gluten-free oat flour
- ½ cup plus 1 teaspoon (63 GRAMS) teff flour
- ⅔ cup (128 GRAMS) potato starch
- ½ cup (60 GRAMS) arrowroot
- 2 tablespoons (12 GRAMS) unsweetened cocoa powder
- 2 teaspoons xanthan gum
- 1 teaspoon baking powder
- 2 teaspoons salt

bread evolution

fresh bread the next day

Gluten-free, vegan breads, free of preservatives and other unseemly ingredients that help fake freshness over time, are delicate. You will find that they need to be eaten the day you prepare them. There are, however, two tricks to get a few extra days' life out of them:

1. Slice, double wrap, and freeze all the baked bread you won't use immediately after it cools. When you're ready for it, toss the bread in the toaster for as long as you desire.

2. Prepare your dough and bake only what you need (in small loaf molds or muffin rings). Wrap the unused dough in plastic wrap and toss it in the refrigerator, where it will keep for up to five days. When you're ready for the next batch, remove the dough from the refrigerator and let it come to room temperature for at least one hour. Remove the plastic wrap and bake as indicated in the recipe, but mind your baking times: They will vary slightly depending on size, obviously.

bread mix-ins

With nearly all of these bread recipes, you can have fun with mix-ins, which are simply ingredients you love, have lying around, and want to experiment with but which are not found in my ingredients list. Here are the rules:

1. Nuts and Seeds: All of your wildest combinations will work structurally, as long as the new ingredients are fresh. The one strict rule, though, is to use no more than ¾ cup of any nut or seed combination in any given recipe.

2. Herbs: Although you can experiment with dried herbs, I find the flavor to be overpowering and a bit . . . corporate?

I don't usually have a single problem with dried herbs, but in these breads, they seem to overpower the love. I avoid them. I do, though, recommend using whatever fresh herbs your heart desires. Just don't use more than 2½ tablespoons total per loaf.

3. Spices: Ground ginger, cayenne pepper, red pepper flakes, and/or a pinch of cinnamon can breathe fiery new life into these breads. Start with a teaspoon of whatever freaky thing sounds good to you and taste the batter until you reach the desired flavor pitch. I recommend going teaspoon by teaspoon because failures are costly.

pumpernickel bread

As a kid I was very fearful of any breads darker than those that are bleached into electric-white submission. Pumpernickel was the most suspect of all given its blackened hue and sinister crust. Had it turned bad? Who left it out too long?

But did you know that pumpernickel is actually kind of sweet and among the most delicious breads out there? True. Of all the breads in this chapter, this makes my favorite toast. Drench it, please, with Butter (page 133). Add a mellow jam or marmalade if you must, but it isn't necessary.

Lightly grease a 7 by 4 by 3-inch loaf pan with oil.

In a small bowl, combine the warm rice milk, agave nectar, and yeast. Stir once and set aside to proof until it bubbles, about 10 minutes.

In a medium bowl, whisk together the flours, ground flaxseed, cocoa powder, sugar, xanthan gum, baking powder, and salt. Pour in the oil, vinegar, applesauce, and the yeast mixture and, using a rubber spatula, stir until it is the consistency of cake batter. If the dough is too thick, add additional warm water one splash at a time. Pour the batter into the prepared loaf pan, cover with a dish towel, and let the dough rise for 1 hour.

Preheat the oven to 400°F.

Bake the bread for 20 minutes, and then rotate the pan 180 degrees. Bake until the crust is golden brown and a toothpick inserted in the center comes out clean, about 15 minutes.

Let the bread cool in the pan for 1 hour before slicing.

2 tablespoons (28 GRAMS) melted unscented coconut oil, plus more for the pan

1½ cups (339 GRAMS) warm rice milk (about 100°F)

1 tablespoon (22 GRAMS) agave nectar

2¼ teaspoons active dry yeast

1¼ cups (175 GRAMS) Bob's Red Mill Gluten-Free All-Purpose Baking Flour

½ cup (50 GRAMS) gluten-free oat flour

2 tablespoons (15 GRAMS) teff flour

¼ cup (28 GRAMS) ground flaxseed (flax meal)

3 tablespoons (18 GRAMS) unsweetened cocoa powder

2 tablespoons vegan sugar

2 teaspoons xanthan gum

1 teaspoon baking powder

1 teaspoon salt

1 teaspoon apple cider vinegar

2 tablespoons (32 GRAMS) unsweetened applesauce

sandwich bread

I worried for a long time over what to call this bread. Is it simply white bread? Is it peasant bread? Ultimately, it is mother to the others in this chapter—it is, in fact, the core of the entire book. Sandwich Bread, as I finally cleverly dubbed it, is as formidable on sandwiches as it is dunked into a bowl of fresh, deep-green olive oil. I use it for French Toast (page 36), croutons, bread salad, and anything else that calls for something absolutely reliable.

Lightly grease a 7 by 4 by 3-inch loaf pan with oil.

In a small bowl, combine the coconut oil, warm water, agave nectar, and yeast. Stir once and set aside until it bubbles, about 10 minutes.

In a large mixing bowl, whisk together the potato starch, flours, arrowroot, baking powder, xanthan gum, and salt. Add the yeast mixture and, using a rubber spatula, stir until it is the consistency of a cake batter. Add more warm water one splash at a time if the batter is too thick. Pour the batter into the prepared loaf pan, cover with a dishtowel, and let rise for 1 hour.

Preheat the oven to 400°F.

Bake the bread for 20 minutes. Rotate the pan 180 degrees and bake until the crust is golden and a toothpick inserted in the center comes out clean, about 15 minutes. Let the bread cool in the pan for 1 hour before slicing.

makes one 7 by 4 by 3-inch loaf

- 2 teaspoons melted unscented coconut oil, plus more for the pan
- 2¼ cups (508 GRAMS) warm water (about 100°F)
- 2½ tablespoons (55 GRAMS) agave nectar
- 2¼ teaspoons active dry yeast
- 1 cup (192 GRAMS) potato starch
- 1 cup (100 GRAMS) gluten-free oat flour
- ¾ cup (90 GRAMS) millet flour
- ½ cup (60 GRAMS) arrowroot
- 1 teaspoon baking powder
- 1½ teaspoons xanthan gum
- 1½ teaspoons salt

**salty-sweet
sesame
bread**

BabyCakes NYC's first shop, on the Lower East Side of Manhattan, is a few steps from Chinatown. In this neighborhood, you can find some of the most fascinating culinary experiences on the planet. I can enjoy only, like, six of them. But when walking by the area's many bakeries, it is impossible to ignore the fleets of golden bun tops that are lined up in the windows like plump and glittery city-dwelling sunbathers. Those beautiful things were on my mind when I was developing this recipe.

Lightly grease a 7 by 4 by 3-inch loaf pan with oil.

In a small bowl, combine 2 tablespoons of the coconut oil, the warm water, 2 tablespoons of the agave nectar, and the yeast. Stir once and set aside to proof until it bubbles, about 10 minutes.

In a medium bowl, whisk together the flours, arrowroot, potato starch, sesame seeds, xanthan gum, baking powder, baking soda, and salt. Add the yeast mixture and, using a rubber spatula, stir until it is the consistency of cake batter. If the dough is too thick, add additional warm water one splash at a time. Pour the dough into the prepared loaf pan, cover with a dish towel, and let the dough rise for 1 hour.

Preheat the oven to 400°F.

In a cup, combine the remaining 2 tablespoons agave nectar and 1 tablespoon oil. Brush the dough with the mixture and sprinkle with salt and additional sesame seeds.

Bake the bread for 20 minutes, and then rotate the pan 180 degrees. Bake until the crust is golden and a toothpick inserted in the center comes out clean, about 15 minutes.

Let the bread cool in the pan for 1 hour before slicing.

makes one 7 by 4 by 3-inch loaf

- 3 tablespoons (42 GRAMS) melted unscented coconut oil, plus more for the pan
- 2 cups (452 GRAMS) warm water (about 100°F)
- ¼ cup (88 GRAMS) agave nectar
- 2¼ teaspoons active dry yeast
- 2¼ cups (225 GRAMS) gluten-free oat flour
- ¼ cup (30 GRAMS) garbanzo–fava bean flour
- ⅓ cup (40 GRAMS) arrowroot
- ⅔ cup (128 GRAMS) potato starch
- ½ cup (65 GRAMS) toasted sesame seeds, plus more for sprinkling
- 2 teaspoons xanthan gum
- 1 teaspoon baking powder
- ¼ teaspoon baking soda
- 2 teaspoons salt, plus more for sprinkling

wrap bread

If you are one of those super-prepared, always-thinking-ahead sorts, this recipe is perfect for you. It is easy to pull together, stores very well in the freezer, and is extremely versatile. Be sure to roll it out thin; it tends to puff up quite a bit during the cooking process. This can also serve as pita bread, if you happen to pull together some falafel balls or the Hummus (page 134). Just roll the dough out as instructed, cut into 8-inch circles, fold into half-moons, seal the sides with your fingertips, and bake!

makes 4

1 cup (140 GRAMS) Bob's Red Mill Gluten-Free All-Purpose Baking Flour

¼ cup (25 GRAMS) gluten-free oat flour

½ cup (60 GRAMS) arrowroot

2 tablespoons (28 GRAMS) vegan sugar

2¼ teaspoons active dry yeast

1 teaspoon xanthan gum

¼ teaspoon baking powder

1 teaspoon salt

¾ cup plus 2 tablespoons (198 GRAMS) room-temperature coconut milk

¼ cup (56 GRAMS) melted unscented coconut oil

In a medium bowl, whisk together the flours, arrowroot, sugar, yeast, xanthan gum, baking powder, and salt. Pour in the coconut milk and oil and, using a rubber spatula, stir until a thick dough forms. If the dough is too dry, add warm water one splash at a time. Wrap the dough in plastic and refrigerate for 1 hour.

Preheat the oven to 325°F. Line a baking sheet with parchment paper and set aside.

Remove the dough from the refrigerator, unwrap it, and place it between 2 pieces of parchment paper. Roll out the dough until it is a rectangle about ¼ inch thick. Remove the parchment paper, slice the dough into 4 equal-size rectangles, and put them on the prepared baking sheet.

Bake the bread until very lightly golden, 10 minutes.

Let the wraps cool on the sheet for 10 minutes before serving.

flax meal bread

Without any justifiable reason other than the fact that all of my recipes have long reaped the rewards of this wonder ingredient, I am very proud of flax meal's success. These last few years ground flaxseed (also known as flax meal) has gone from a relatively obscure little health-based ingredient to a fully recognizable and branded mass-market success. I use it often, but usually in small doses. Until this recipe, that is! The mega fiber and omega-3s from the flax, combined with chia seeds, should make this your go-to bread when you're feeling bad about overindulging at the dessert station.

Lightly grease a 7 by 4 by 3-inch loaf pan with oil.

In a small bowl, combine the warm water, agave nectar, and yeast. Stir once and set aside to proof until it bubbles, about 10 minutes.

In a medium bowl, whisk together the flours, arrowroot, potato starch, ground flaxseed, chia seeds, xanthan gum, baking powder, baking soda, and salt. Pour in the oil, applesauce, and yeast mixture and, using a rubber spatula, stir until it is the consistency of cake batter. If the dough is too thick, add additional warm water one splash at a time. Pour the dough into the prepared loaf pan, cover with a dish towel, and let the dough rise for 1 hour.

Preheat the oven to 400°F.

Bake the bread for 20 minutes, and then rotate the pan 180 degrees. Bake until the crust is lightly golden and a toothpick inserted in the center comes out clean, about 15 minutes. Let the bread cool in the pan for 1 hour before slicing.

makes one 7 by 4 by 3-inch loaf

2 tablespoons (28 GRAMS) melted unscented coconut oil, plus more for the pan

1½ cups (339 GRAMS) warm water (about 100°F)

2 tablespoons (44 GRAMS) agave nectar

2¼ teaspoons active dry yeast

1 cup (140 GRAMS) Bob's Red Mill Gluten-Free All-Purpose Baking Flour

¾ cup (75 GRAMS) gluten-free oat flour

¼ cup (30 GRAMS) teff flour

½ cup (60 GRAMS) arrowroot

⅓ cup (64 GRAMS) potato starch

¼ cup (28 GRAMS) ground flaxseed (flax meal)

¼ cup (41 GRAMS) chia seeds

1 teaspoon xanthan gum

1 teaspoon baking powder

¼ teaspoon baking soda

2 teaspoons salt

1 tablespoon (16 GRAMS) unsweetened applesauce

spicy vegetable cornbread

At the bakery we are all constantly barraged with requests for this recipe, which is so flattering and impossibly sweet and undeniably charming. But at the same time, I'm eager to get this recipe in your hands so we can get back to talking about what I should do next with my hair.

Preheat the oven to 325°F. Lightly grease a 7 by 4 by 3-inch loaf pan with oil.

Pour the rice milk and vinegar into a small bowl, but do not stir; set the mixture aside to develop into a buttermilk.

In a medium bowl, whisk together the flours, cornmeal, baking powder, baking soda, xanthan gum, red pepper flakes, and salt. Pour in the oil, agave nectar, applesauce, and vanilla and, using a rubber spatula, stir well. Pour in the buttermilk. Stir gently until a slightly grainy batter is formed. Fold in the onion, zucchini, and broccoli. Pour the dough into the prepared loaf pan. Sprinkle the black pepper over the top.

Bake the cornbread for 30 minutes, and then rotate the pan 180 degrees. Bake until the crust is golden and a toothpick inserted in the center comes out clean, 10 to 12 minutes. Let the bread cool in the pan for 30 minutes before slicing.

makes one 7 by 4 by 3-inch loaf

½ cup (112 GRAMS) melted unscented coconut oil, plus more for the pan

⅔ cup (150 GRAMS) rice milk

1 tablespoon (15 GRAMS) apple cider vinegar

¾ cup (105 GRAMS) Bob's Red Mill Gluten-Free All-Purpose Baking Flour

½ cup (58 GRAMS) corn flour

½ cup (66 GRAMS) cornmeal

2 teaspoons baking powder

1 teaspoon baking soda

1 teaspoon xanthan gum

1 teaspoon crushed red pepper flakes

1 teaspoon salt

½ cup (176 GRAMS) agave nectar

⅓ cup (80 GRAMS) unsweetened applesauce

1 teaspoon pure vanilla extract

¼ onion, chopped fine

½ zucchini, chopped

¼ cup (23 GRAMS) broccoli florets, halved

Freshly cracked black pepper

carrot bread

In each of my bakeries, carrot cupcakes are best sellers. No doubt this is because of the incredible moistness and subtle sweetness carrots provide. In order to make this bread I used the same ratio of carrots to flour that I do in a cake batter, but I reduced both the sugar and the fat to give it a lighter, more airy crumb. I especially like to make this recipe with walnut oil, but coconut oil is absolutely perfect as well.

3 tablespoons (39 GRAMS) walnut oil or melted unscented coconut oil, plus more for the pan

1½ cups (339 GRAMS) warm water (about 100°F)

4 tablespoons (56 GRAMS) vegan sugar

2¼ teaspoons active dry yeast

2 cups (280 GRAMS) Bob's Red Mill Gluten-Free All-Purpose Baking Flour

2 tablespoons (15 GRAMS) arrowroot

½ teaspoon xanthan gum

1 teaspoon baking powder

2 teaspoons ground cinnamon

¼ teaspoon ground nutmeg

1½ teaspoons salt

2 cups (254 GRAMS) firmly packed shredded carrots

¾ cup (96 GRAMS) chopped walnuts (optional)

Lightly grease a 7 by 4 by 3-inch loaf pan with oil.

In a small bowl, combine the oil, warm water, sugar, and yeast. Stir once and set aside to proof until it bubbles, about 10 minutes.

In a medium bowl, whisk together the flour, arrowroot, xanthan gum, baking powder, cinnamon, nutmeg, and salt. Pour in the yeast mixture and, using a rubber spatula, stir until it is the consistency of cake batter. If the dough is too thick, add additional warm water one splash at a time. Fold in the carrots and the walnuts (if using). Pour the dough into the prepared loaf pan, cover with a dish towel, and let the dough rise for 1 hour.

Preheat the oven to 400°F.

Bake the bread for 20 minutes, and then rotate the pan 180 degrees. Bake until the crust is golden and a toothpick inserted in the center comes out clean, about 15 minutes.

Let the bread cool in the pan for 1 hour before slicing.

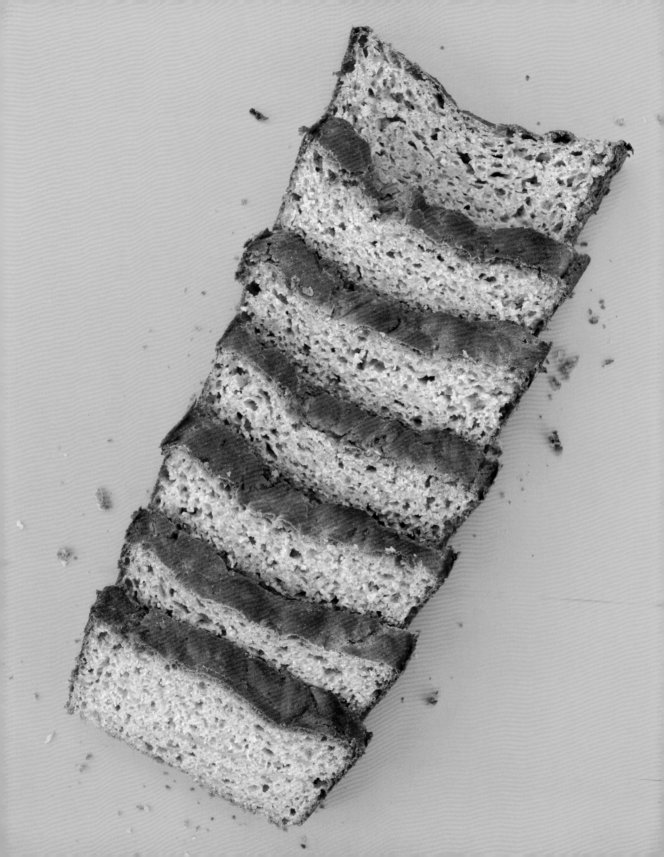

sweet potato and sage pull-apart rolls

Although these rolls make a nice year-round addition to dinnertime, they were actually created for your Thanksgiving table. You can use fresh sweet potatoes and mash them up for this recipe to give it even more depth of flavor, and if sage is not your thing, both rosemary and thyme are excellent substitutes.

Line a baking sheet with parchment paper, dust with cornmeal, and set aside.

In a small bowl, combine the warm rice milk, agave nectar, and yeast. Stir once and set aside to proof until it bubbles, about 10 minutes. Whisk in the oil and sweet potato.

In a medium bowl, whisk together the oat flour, potato starch, baking powder, baking soda, xanthan gum, and salt. Pour in the yeast mixture and, using a rubber spatula, stir until it is the consistency of a sticky dough. Fold in the sage.

Using a ½-cup measuring cup, scoop heaping portions of batter onto the prepared baking sheet and shape into squares. Leave no more than ½ inch between each roll on the pan. Cover the baking sheet with a dish towel and let the rolls rise for 1 hour.

Preheat the oven to 400°F.

Bake the rolls for 10 minutes, and then rotate the baking sheet 180 degrees. Bake until the crust is golden and a toothpick inserted in the center comes out clean, about 6 minutes. Let the rolls cool on the pan for 10 minutes before serving.

makes 12

¼ cup (33 GRAMS) **cornmeal, for the baking sheet**

1½ cups (339 GRAMS) **warm rice milk (about 100°F)**

3 tablespoons (66 GRAMS) **agave nectar**

2½ teaspoons **active dry yeast**

⅓ cup (70 GRAMS) **melted unscented coconut oil**

½ cup (165 GRAMS) **canned sweet potato puree (at room temperature)**

3 cups (300 GRAMS) **gluten-free oat flour**

½ cup (96 GRAMS) **potato starch**

1 teaspoon **baking powder**

¼ teaspoon **baking soda**

1½ teaspoons **xanthan gum**

2 teaspoons **salt**

⅓ cup (9 GRAMS) **sage leaves, chopped**

seeded rolls

I clumped three seeds together because they all cook at more or less the same rate and together they make each bite of this bread a multilayered experience. The beauty of these rolls is (a) that you use whatever you have in the pantry, and (b) seeds lend such a fun aftertaste. Also (c) these things can keep my daughter occupied for at least twenty minutes as she chases the escaped seedlings around the kitchen table with her tiny fingertips. I'll take a twenty-minute break wherever and however it is available.

makes 8

4 teaspoons (18 GRAMS) melted unscented coconut oil, plus more for brushing the baking sheet

1¼ cups (282 GRAMS) warm water (about 100°F)

2 tablespoons (44 GRAMS) agave nectar

2¼ teaspoons active dry yeast

1½ cups minus 2 tablespoons (138 GRAMS) gluten-free oat flour

1 cup minus 2 tablespoons (105 GRAMS) teff flour

¼ cup (48 GRAMS) potato starch

¼ cup (18 GRAMS) poppy seeds

¼ cup (40 GRAMS) sesame seeds

2 tablespoons (22 GRAMS) chia seeds

2 tablespoons (14 GRAMS) ground flaxseed (flax meal)

2 tablespoons (28 GRAMS) vegan sugar

1 teaspoon baking powder

1 teaspoon xanthan gum

1 teaspoon salt

4 teaspoons (80 GRAMS) apple cider vinegar

Line a baking sheet with parchment paper, brush parchment with oil, and set aside.

In a small bowl, combine the warm water, agave nectar, and yeast. Stir once and set aside to proof until it bubbles, about 10 minutes.

In a medium bowl, whisk together the flours, potato starch, poppy seeds, sesame seeds, chia seeds, ground flaxseed, sugar, baking powder, xanthan gum, and salt. Pour in the oil, vinegar, and the yeast mixture and, using a rubber spatula, stir until it is the consistency of cake batter. If the dough is too thick, add additional warm water one splash at a time.

Using a ½-cup measuring cup, scoop heaping portions of the dough onto the prepared baking sheet without fussing with them. Cover the baking sheet with a dish towel and let the rolls rise for 1 hour.

Preheat the oven to 400°F.

Bake the rolls for 10 minutes, and then rotate the baking sheet 180 degrees. Bake until they are golden and a toothpick inserted in the center comes out clean, about 4 minutes. Let the rolls cool on the sheet for 10 minutes before serving.

sandwiches

It will come as no surprise to you that the ability to prepare a
sandwich was a motivating factor in the development of this book
of mostly savory bread recipes. All you working allergy-restricted
adults understand, I'm sure, that sometimes it just isn't possible to
run down the lunch of your dreams, and there are days when you'll
make do with anything to get to the end of the day. But frankly, I'm
bored with the expensive and humiliating experience of ordering
a sandwich at a restaurant simply to eat its insides, which until
recently has happened far too often.

    The sandwiches that follow are some of my favorites, though
there is no ceiling to what we can do here. I added a simple Cucumber
Tea Sandwich (page 67) to illustrate something delicious that you
can muster with next to nothing in the fridge. There are also a
few recipes—Roasted Fennel Sandwich with White Bean Spread
(page 66), for example—that are a bit more detailed but that I've
come to love as a deep-space exploration of what is possible now
that we have bread.

vegetable club sandwich

I set out to make my version of the classic club and here's where I landed: kale, eggplant, avocado, and tomatoes. Trust me, this is one of those recipes that works even if it sounds like it shouldn't. Best I can tell, it is the kale chips that push this thing over the top into glory-land. Don't scrimp on them during assembly.

serves 6

2 tablespoons (28 GRAMS) melted unscented coconut oil or olive oil

2 garlic cloves, minced

½ eggplant, peeled and cut into ½-inch-thick slices

6 Seeded Rolls (page 58)

6 tablespoons (84 GRAMS) Mayonnaise (page 131)

1 medium tomato, sliced

1 avocado, sliced

Kale Chips (page 126)

Salt and freshly ground black pepper

Line a large plate with paper towels and set aside.

Heat 1 teaspoon of the oil in a wide skillet set over low heat. Add the garlic and cook, stirring gently, until lightly browned, 1 to 1½ minutes. Transfer the garlic to a small bowl.

Add the remaining oil to the skillet, then add the eggplant slices and cook until they are browned on the bottom, about 3 minutes. Flip the slices over and cook until the second side is browned and the eggplant is soft, about 2 more minutes. Transfer the eggplant to the paper towel–lined plate.

Cut the seeded rolls in half and spread each side with mayonnaise. Put 2 slices of eggplant on each of the bottom halves of the rolls. Top each with garlic, 2 slices of tomato, 4 slices of avocado, and 3 pieces of kale; season with salt and pepper. Top with the roll tops. Serve immediately.

the smashed grilled cheese

The art of the grilled cheese sandwich is passed down from generation to generation, each person building her own style and methodology on the shoulders of her forebearers and bringing it to the stovetop. I won't pretend that I am your rule-toting chaperone on this voyage. I'll just offer two quick notes: 1. BabyCakes bread, probably because of its heavy reliance on coconut oil, has a delightful way of melding with the cheese, so your go-to cheese selection may require some rethinking. 2. The Butter crisps sandwiches into something a bit lighter than the occasionally chewy ones I remember from my youth (both a warning and a celebration!).

Spread one side of each slice of bread with butter.

Heat a cast-iron or nonstick skillet over medium heat. Put one piece of buttered bread, butter side down, in the skillet. Pile ½ cup of cheese on the bread, put a second slice of buttered bread on top, with the buttered side up, and cook until golden brown, about 1½ minutes. Flip the sandwich over and put a heavy pan on top of the sandwich to squish it. Cook until the second slice of bread is golden brown, another 1½ minutes. Transfer the sandwich to a cutting board and, using a pizza cutter, cut the sandwich in half diagonally. Repeat with the remaining ingredients. Serve immediately.

serves 6

1 loaf Sandwich Bread (page 47), cut into 12 (½-inch-thick) slices

¼ cup (56 GRAMS) Butter (page 133), softened

3 cups (339 GRAMS) grated vegan gluten-free cheese (I prefer Daiya or Teese)

avocado and arugula sandwich with walnut spread

The grocery store is my sanctuary. I often wander in knowing full well that there is nothing I need, simply to stroll the aisles. One recent aimless visit I stumbled onto walnut oil, something I'd never heard of before that moment. So I forked over my $19,143.08 (more or less) and I brought home the tiny, beautiful can. Whoa! It was a revelation. This recipe does not call for walnut oil, because it is too pricey for me to list it in good conscience (at home I divvy it up to myself in tiny weekly rations to make it last). Instead, this is my mock version of walnut oil, built as a spread, but capturing all the nutty richness I love most about it.

In a small skillet set over medium heat, toast the walnuts, shaking occasionally, until browned and fragrant, about 1 minute. Remove the nuts from the heat, let cool, and chop.

In a food processor, combine the navy beans, ¾ cup of the toasted walnuts, 2 tablespoons of the olive oil, the lemon juice, and the garlic and puree until smooth. Transfer the spread to a small bowl, add the salt, season with pepper, and fold in the remaining walnuts.

Slice two pieces of carrot bread. Spread a heaping tablespoon of the walnut spread on each slice. Top one side with arugula, avocado, a drizzle of olive oil, a dash of lemon juice, and salt and pepper to taste. Close and serve.

serves 6

WALNUT SPREAD
1 cup (100 GRAMS) walnuts

½ (15-ounce) can (212 GRAMS) navy beans, drained

2 tablespoons (28 GRAMS) olive oil, plus more for drizzling

1 tablespoon (15 GRAMS) fresh lemon juice

1 garlic clove, minced

½ teaspoon (3 GRAMS) salt

Freshly ground black pepper

Carrot Bread (page 54)

2 cups (40 GRAMS) fresh arugula

1 ripe avocado, sliced

2 tablespoons (30 GRAMS) fresh lemon juice

Salt and freshly ground black pepper

the sandwich bar

For the second time in my life, I am new to making sandwiches (the first time was circa 1983). But in writing this book I cast a very wide net to find which sandwiches were my favorites. Those that I like best got their own page, but there are a few that I just couldn't shake. And, so, here are a few more ideas for using all that bread you've made.

Monte Cristo: Follow the French Toast recipe (page 36), adding a handful of vegan cheese (of them all, I prefer those made by Daiya) and a few slices of either a roasted vegetable or a fake meat (whatever you're into). Cook as instructed and serve.

The Anything Parm: Whip up some bread crumbs using a day-old bread, lightly bread your favorite hearty vegetable (eggplant and portobello mushrooms are obviously perfect), and fry in oil on the stovetop until crisp. On a baking sheet, place 2 thick slices of bread and top each with the vegetables, a liberal dose of Pizza Sauce (page 74), and a small handful of vegan cheese and bake in a preheated oven at 350°F for 10 minutes or until the cheese melts. Close the sandwich and enjoy!

Grilled Cheese Croissant: Slice the croissant open. Sprinkle with a good bit of vegan cheese, close the sandwich, and grill in a small sauté pan set over medium heat for 3 minutes on each side, or until the cheese inside melts.

roasted fennel sandwich
with white bean spread

I can indulge once in a while, right? This recipe is about as fancy as I get, with as many un-sweet steps as I'm comfortable assigning you. It's not even that much work, though, come on! If you'd like to mess around with other roasted vegetables in place of the fennel, I find that sturdy vegetables like squash and eggplant work very well.

Preheat the oven to 400°F. Line a rimmed baking sheet with parchment paper and set aside.

Arrange the fennel slices on the prepared baking sheet. Drizzle with the olive oil and lemon juice and sprinkle with salt and pepper. Bake until tender, 20 minutes. Let cool on the sheet for 15 minutes.

Make the white bean spread: Heat the oil in a wide skillet set over medium heat. Add the onion and cook, stirring, until tender, about 3 minutes. Add the garlic and cook, stirring, for 1 minute. Remove the skillet from the heat and let the mixture cool in the skillet for 5 minutes.

In a food processor, combine the onion mixture, beans, lemon juice, rosemary, and cayenne and season to taste with salt and pepper. Pulse until the mixture is smooth but still slightly coarse.

To serve, spread a heaping tablespoon of the white bean spread over each piece of sliced bread. Put the fennel on half of the bread slices, sprinkle with a small pinch of salt and black pepper, top with the remaining bread slices, and serve.

serves 6

2 medium fennel bulbs, trimmed, cored, and sliced

3 tablespoons (42 GRAMS) olive oil

1 tablespoon (15 GRAMS) lemon juice

Salt and freshly ground black pepper

WHITE BEAN SPREAD

2 tablespoons (28 GRAMS) olive oil

¼ small yellow onion, chopped

2 garlic cloves, chopped

1 (15-OUNCE; 425-GRAM) can white beans, drained

3 tablespoons (45 GRAMS) fresh lemon juice

1 tablespoon (2 GRAMS) chopped fresh rosemary

½ teaspoon cayenne pepper or crushed red pepper flakes

Salt and freshly ground black pepper

12 slices of the bread of your choice

cucumber tea sandwich

This sandwich is an excellent example of how perfection is often found in simplicity. It is delicate and light, and it plays as much on texture as it does on flavor. Buttered, untoasted bread is one of humankind's truly great accomplishments.

In a medium bowl, sprinkle the cucumber ribbons lightly with salt, toss gently, and set aside.

Spread a spoonful of butter on one side of each slice of bread and fold a quarter of the cucumber in layers on one slice. Place some of the dill on top of the cucumber and sprinkle with salt and pepper. Place the other slice of bread on top, remove the crusts with a knife, and quarter the sandwich into equal squares. Continue until all the sandwiches are assembled.

serves 4

1 English cucumber, peeled and shaved into ribbons

Salt

4 tablespoons (56 GRAMS) Butter (page 133), softened

8 slices Sandwich Bread (page 47)

1½ teaspoons snipped fresh dill

Freshly ground black pepper

pizza and focaccia

To avoid disagreement let's just assume that there is a single platonic ideal of pizza crust. It veers thin but is not a cracker. Its texture is chewy though not doughy, and it can tolerate up to a couple of standard-issue toppings without being ruined. It is simple and perfect.

Jim Lahey, of Sullivan Street Bakery in New York, is among this pizza crust's modern masters, as are the most venerable NYC pizza houses, old and new: Coney Island's Totonno's, John's of Bleecker Street in Manhattan, and Roberta's in Brooklyn, especially. The gluten-free among us have likely never tried crusts like these (maybe several of you vegans haven't either).

The Pizza Dough on page 70 came about—you guessed it—by accident, as I was testing the three hundredth version of the gluten-free croissant. I recklessly threw my usual ingredients into the bowl, rolled it out, and put it in the oven. Minutes later I realized I had forgotten to add the butter I'd created. As a croissant it was a disaster, but the flavor and texture were unmistakably crust-like. I scribbled down a few changes to the recipe, ran a few tests, and here we are. Welcome to the pizza party.

pizza dough

Flour, water, salt, yeast: For most pizza dough, that's it. Say you have hypothetically had twenty pieces of pizza in your life: How many were terrible? My guess is that eleven were terrible. It is so easy to do it wrong. But you ate those slices down aggressively all the same, paying no mind, because it's pizza. We love pizza. Later, though, maybe you paid deeply for your indulgence, curled up tight in your bed with abdominal anxiety, because gluten has no reciprocal affection for you. I love simplicity as much as the next baker, but for me to get a respectable dough taking all dietary restrictions to heart, things necessarily got a bit more . . . involved. But we made it. Let's do it.

makes one 12-inch pizza crust

1 cup (226 GRAMS) **warm rice milk (about 100°F)**

2 tablespoons (28 GRAMS) **vegan sugar**

2¼ teaspoons **active dry yeast**

¾ cup (144 GRAMS) **potato starch**

½ cup plus 3 tablespoons (112 GRAMS) **brown rice flour**

½ cup plus 1 tablespoon (68 GRAMS) **arrowroot**

2 teaspoons **salt**

1 teaspoon **xanthan gum**

⅓ cup (70 GRAMS) **melted unscented coconut oil**

In a small bowl, combine the warm rice milk, sugar, and yeast. Stir once and set aside until it bubbles, about 10 minutes.

In a medium bowl, whisk together the potato starch, rice flour, arrowroot, salt, and xanthan gum. Add the coconut oil and yeast mixture and, using a rubber spatula, stir until a thick dough forms. Wrap the dough in plastic wrap and refrigerate it for 2 hours.

whole-grain pizza dough

This here's a hippie recipe for all my lovely hippie friends. I've swapped whole-grain oat flour for the rice flour I used in the recipe for Pizza Dough (opposite) and added omega-3-rich flax meal to make it slightly more nutritious for your hippie babies. Because of these new ingredients, this dough is chewier than the basic recipe, but it's really delicious because of that quality. To get a bit of extra crunch to your pizza, sprinkle the baking sheet with cornmeal, sesame seeds, or poppy seeds before baking.

In a small bowl, combine the warm rice milk, sugar, and yeast. Stir once and set aside to proof until it bubbles, about 10 minutes.

In a medium bowl, whisk together the oat flour, potato starch, arrowroot, ground flaxseed, salt, and xanthan gum. Add the coconut oil and yeast mixture and, using a rubber spatula, stir until a thick dough forms. Wrap the dough in plastic wrap and refrigerate for 2 hours.

---

makes one 12-inch pizza crust

1 cup (226 GRAMS) warm rice milk (about 100°F)

2 tablespoons (28 GRAMS) vegan sugar

2¼ teaspoons active dry yeast

1 cup (100 GRAMS) gluten-free oat flour

½ cup minus 1 tablespoon (84 GRAMS) potato starch

½ cup (60 GRAMS) arrowroot

2½ tablespoons (18 GRAMS) ground flaxseed (flax meal)

1 teaspoon salt

1 teaspoon xanthan gum

¼ cup (56 GRAMS) melted unscented coconut oil

roasted vegetable pizza

My bakery's pantry reveals that I am mostly a straight shooter: chocolate, vanilla, cinnamon, salt, fruit, vegetables. We do have the occasional elaborate flavor combo indulgence, sure, but mostly it is a purist enterprise. But of course, many of you are out for knowledge, and I appreciate that. So to scratch that itch, I tested out a bunch of methods for putting some of my favorite vegetables on pizza dough. As always, if you can spare it, those extra few bucks you spend at the produce market are worth it.

Preheat the oven to 450°F.

Trim the ends off the zucchini and eggplant and discard. Using a vegetable peeler, peel the zucchini lengthwise to create ribbons. Put the zucchini in a bowl and toss with the lemon juice and ½ teaspoon salt. Using a knife, slice the eggplant into thin rings. Put the eggplant in a separate small bowl and coat with the olive oil. Let both sit for 30 minutes.

Between 2 pieces of parchment paper, roll out the pizza dough into a circle about ¼ inch thick and 12 inches in diameter. Transfer the dough and bottom parchment to a baking sheet. Spread the pizza sauce over the dough, beginning in the center and working in circles outward, and layer it with the zucchini, eggplant (including the oil from the eggplant), and olives. Drizzle with additional oil, top with the basil, and season with salt and pepper.

Bake for 15 minutes, and then rotate the sheet 180 degrees. Bake until the bottom is browned and crispy, 10 minutes. Let the pizza cool on the baking sheet for 5 minutes before serving.

serves 10

1 medium zucchini

½ medium eggplant

2 tablespoons (30 GRAMS) fresh lemon juice

Coarse salt and freshly ground black pepper

¼ cup (56 GRAMS) olive oil, plus more for drizzling

Pizza Dough (page 70) or Whole-Grain Pizza Dough (page 71)

1½ cups (189 GRAMS) Pizza Sauce (page 74)

¼ cup (50 GRAMS) black olives, chopped

⅓ cup (12 GRAMS) fresh basil leaves, torn

pizza sauce

You probably have your own recipe for this. Or maybe there is a jarred version you love or that your kids love. This is mine—or at least the one I have subconsciously developed from similar recipes ingredient by ingredient over the years. It's almost embarrassingly simple.

Heat the oil in a wide skillet set over medium heat. Add the onion and garlic and cook, stirring occasionally, until lightly browned, about 3 minutes. Add the tomatoes, basil, and red pepper flakes, and season with salt and pepper to taste. Bring the sauce to a boil, reduce the heat to low, and simmer for 10 minutes. That's it. That's my recipe. Ta-da!

makes 3½ cups

2 tablespoons (28 GRAMS) olive oil

¼ small yellow onion, chopped

2 garlic cloves, minced

1 (28-ounce) can crushed tomatoes

½ teaspoon dried basil

½ teaspoon crushed red pepper flakes

Coarse salt and freshly ground black pepper

pizza biscuits

For most office-dwelling people I know, the cost of having good health benefits and bank holidays off is that "lunch" means having something delivered to your desk so as not to miss even one minute of the hot business action. I'm no exception, except my office happens to be in the basement of a bakery. To make missing lunch tolerable, I stuff small snacks into my bag until nothing else can fit. In order to make sure there is guaranteed space, a pizza biscuit is the first thing I add.

makes 12

1 recipe dough for Biscuits (page 24)

¼ small yellow onion, chopped

6 cherry tomatoes, halved

1½ teaspoons crushed red pepper flakes

1 teaspoon dried oregano

Salt and freshly ground black pepper

1½ cups (170 GRAMS) grated or shredded vegan gluten-free cheese (I prefer Daiya or Teese)

2 tablespoons (28 GRAMS) melted unscented coconut oil

Preheat the oven to 375°F. Line a baking sheet with parchment paper and set aside.

Put the biscuit dough in a large bowl.

In a medium bowl, toss together the onion, tomatoes, red pepper flakes, and oregano, and season with salt. Add the vegetable mixture and the cheese to the biscuit dough and stir until well incorporated.

Transfer the dough to a piece of parchment paper. Using your hands, push the dough out into a circle or rectangle about 2 inches thick. Using a 3-inch cookie cutter, cut out the biscuits and put them on the prepared sheet about 1 inch apart. Brush the biscuits with coconut oil and sprinkle the tops with salt and pepper.

Bake for 12 minutes, and then rotate the baking sheet 180 degrees. Bake until the biscuits are cooked through and the outsides are golden brown, 6 to 8 minutes. Remove the biscuits from the oven and let cool for 5 minutes before serving.

pizza
with a salad
on top

This one is straight out of 1996. I woke up one morning, perhaps a tiny bit hungover in the college sense of the word, and suddenly all the pizzas in the world were covered with salads. They *all* had Hidden Valley Ranch as their dressing, and I didn't mind! They sold for $5.99, which was always $4.99 more than I had, but eventually I scrimped and saved up enough to get one. It was at Blondie's Pizza in San Francisco. I ate it and loved it. And then I went home and suffered, like I always did back then, well before I knew that gluten was secretly making my life painful. As soon as I managed to get the pizza dough recipe all worked out, I put a salad together, plopped it on top, and ate it. I love you, 1996.

4 cups (596 GRAMS) sliced cherry tomatoes

3 tablespoons (42 GRAMS) olive oil

2 garlic cloves, minced

3 tablespoons (2 GRAMS) fresh oregano leaves, torn

Coarse salt and freshly ground black pepper

Pizza Dough (page 70) or Whole-Grain Pizza Dough (page 71)

2 cups (40 GRAMS) arugula

¼ cup (40 GRAMS) thinly sliced red onion

3 tablespoons (45 GRAMS) red wine vinegar

Preheat the oven to 450°F.

Put all but ½ cup of the tomatoes into a medium bowl. Drizzle in 2 tablespoons of the olive oil. Add the garlic, toss in the oregano, and season with salt and pepper to taste. Mix gently and set aside.

Between 2 pieces of parchment paper, roll out the pizza dough into a circle about ¼ inch thick and 12 inches in diameter. Transfer the dough and bottom parchment to a baking sheet. Top the pizza dough with the tomato mixture in an even layer.

Bake for 20 minutes, and then rotate the sheet 180 degrees. Bake until the crust is browned and crisp, 15 minutes.

In a small bowl, combine the arugula, red onion, and remaining ½ cup tomatoes. Drizzle in the vinegar and remaining 1 tablespoon oil, season with salt and pepper, and toss gently. Arrange the salad on top of the pizza and serve immediately.

focaccia
in the style of italy

Before I opened BabyCakes I was, among other things, a waitress. The highlight of that career was working at Lupa, a Mario Batali restaurant in Manhattan then helmed by chef Mark Ladner, the genius now at New York City's four-star Del Posto. Every day his staff pumped out sheet after sheet of the most beautiful focaccia known to man, as the waitstaff ogled it like sad hungry puppies. But nobody gawked more than I did: By then my gluten sensitivity was in full bloom and focaccia was completely forbidden. This recipe is for all those sheets that passed me by, and have passed you by as well.

Line 2 rimmed baking sheets with parchment paper. Sprinkle one with the cornmeal and set it aside.

Pour the coconut oil onto the other parchment-lined baking sheet and refrigerate for 30 minutes. The oil will harden into a thin, solid sheet that will be broken into pieces later.

In a large bowl, whisk together the potato starch, flours, arrowroot, sugar, baking powder, salt, yeast, and xanthan gum. Add the lukewarm coconut milk and rice milk and, using a rubber spatula, stir until the dough pulls away easily from the sides of the bowl. If the dough is too thin, add 1 tablespoon arrowroot at a time. If the dough is too dry, add a splash of lukewarm water.

serves 10

¼ cup (33 GRAMS) cornmeal

½ cup (112 GRAMS) melted unscented coconut oil, plus more for brushing the baking sheet

1⅓ cups (256 GRAMS) potato starch

1 cup (140 GRAMS) brown rice flour

¾ cup (75 GRAMS) gluten-free oat flour

1 cup minus 1 tablespoon (112 GRAMS) arrowroot, or more if needed

2 tablespoons (28 GRAMS) vegan sugar

1 tablespoon (15 GRAMS) baking powder

2 teaspoons salt

2¼ teaspoons active dry yeast

2 teaspoons xanthan gum

1 cup (240 GRAMS) lukewarm coconut milk

½ cup (113 GRAMS) lukewarm rice milk

Transfer the dough to the cornmeal-lined baking sheet and gently spread it out with your fingertips until the dough is about 1 inch thick and has distinct fingerprint dimples throughout. Brush the dough with oil, cover with a dish towel, and let it rise for 1 hour.

Preheat the oven to 400°F.

Remove the hardened coconut oil from the refrigerator and break it into pieces approximately ½ inch in width. Put the coconut oil shards in each dimple in the dough. If there are pieces left over, push them randomly into the dough.

Bake for 15 minutes, and then rotate the baking sheet 180 degrees. Bake until the crust is golden brown, 10 minutes. Remove the focaccia from the oven and let cool for 15 minutes before cutting.

To some, eating too much white food is scary, and I totally get that. When I'm feeling like I want to get some added nutrition credit I make this recipe, which includes a lot of fiber and whole grain but is still salty and chewy and doused with oil. It's a personal favorite. Then I have an extra cookie for dessert.

serves 10

½ cup (112 GRAMS) melted unscented coconut oil, plus more for brushing the baking sheet

2 cups (200 GRAMS) gluten-free oat flour

1 cup plus 1 tablespoon (204 GRAMS) potato starch

¾ cup (90 GRAMS) arrowroot, or more if needed

3 tablespoons (21 GRAMS) ground flaxseed (flax meal)

1 tablespoon (15 GRAMS) baking powder

2 teaspoons salt

2¼ teaspoons active dry yeast

1 teaspoon xanthan gum

2 tablespoons (44 GRAMS) agave nectar

½ cup (120 GRAMS) lukewarm coconut milk

1 cup (226 GRAMS) lukewarm rice milk

Line 2 rimmed baking sheets with parchment paper and set aside.

Pour the coconut oil onto one of the prepared baking sheets and refrigerate for 30 minutes. The oil will harden into a thin, solid sheet that will be broken into pieces later.

In a large bowl, whisk together the flour, potato starch, arrowroot, ground flaxseed, baking powder, salt, yeast, and xanthan gum. Add the agave nectar and lukewarm milks, and, using a rubber spatula, stir until the dough pulls away easily from the sides of the bowl. If the dough is too thin, add 1 tablespoon arrowroot at a time. If the dough is too dry, add a splash of lukewarm water.

Transfer the dough to the second prepared baking sheet and gently spread it out with your fingertips until the dough is about 1 inch thick and has deep fingerprint dimples throughout. Brush the dough with oil, cover with a dish towel, and let rise for 1 hour.

Preheat the oven to 400°F.

Remove the hardened coconut oil from the refrigerator and break it into pieces approximately ½ inch in width. Put the coconut oil shards in each dimple in the dough. If there are pieces left over, push them randomly into the dough.

Bake for 15 minutes, and then rotate the sheet 180 degrees. Bake until the crust is golden brown, 5 minutes. Remove the focaccia from the oven and let cool for 15 minutes before cutting.

focaccia
in the style of the hippies

focaccia
with onion, rosemary, and thyme

Your boss is coming over for dinner. Or maybe it's that neighbor woman you dislike but who is still kind of a pal and whose husband is friendly with your husband and her husband is better than all your husband's other lame friends and you want to foster their relationship. You decide that hosting is a better idea than going to her house. You need something cheap and easy but glitzy enough that you don't look lazy or like a grouch. This is the recipe for you.

serves 10

½ small yellow onion, sliced

¼ cup (52 GRAMS) melted unscented coconut oil

Salt and freshly ground black pepper

1 recipe dough for Focaccia in the Style of Italy (page 78)

2 garlic cloves, minced

Leaves from 1 sprig rosemary (1 TEASPOON)

Leaves from 1 sprig thyme (1½ TEASPOONS)

Preheat the oven to 400°F. Line a baking sheet with parchment paper and set aside.

In a medium bowl, toss the onions with 2 tablespoons of the oil and a pinch of salt. Spread the onions on the prepared baking sheet and roast until they are golden, 20 minutes. Let cool for 10 minutes.

Spread the onions evenly over the prepared focaccia dough, brush with the remaining oil, and sprinkle the garlic, rosemary, thyme, and salt and pepper over the top.

Bake for 15 minutes, and then rotate the sheet 180 degrees. Bake until the crust is golden, 10 minutes. Let the focaccia cool in the pan for 15 minutes before cutting.

this is for the kids

I have a daughter now! She is two and a half, shares none of my dietary complications, and loves to stare deep inside the dishwasher for . . . something. The point is: I'm learning how to keep a child entertained in the kitchen.

What I'm finding is that kids are really just adults who are not bound by all those irritating rules we're encouraged to live by as actual adults. When they want to scream, they scream. If they don't like something, they throw it on the ground. The way to deal with people like this, young or old, is often with sweets and/or cheese. This chapter has plenty of both.

Here you'll find a fun method for sweetening up bananas and bundling them into doughy little sleep sacks. There are Potato and Cauliflower Tots (page 92), my Cheez-It knockoff, and the almighty quesadilla. There is also a Butter and Jelly Bread (page 90) that, no joke, I've been making every week since developing the recipe. You are going to love it. And maybe, just maybe, it'll bring your household blissful, if temporary, silence.

cheese-its

I'll say right up front that I was unable to replicate the electric-orange hue found in this cracker's namesake. I did manage to zero in on that sharp and salty taste, though! Mine is a bit nearer a cheese crisp—a little chewy at times, a bit crispy at others. Want it cheesier? Reduce the flour by half, but know that they will end up quite chewy (not a bad thing!).

Preheat the oven to 375°F. Line a baking sheet with parchment paper and set aside.

In a medium bowl, whisk together the flours, potato starch, cornmeal, sugar, xanthan gum, and salt. Add the oil, agave nectar, and cold water and, using a rubber spatula, stir until a thick dough forms. Add the cheese and work it into the dough with your hands until it is evenly distributed. Wrap the dough in plastic wrap and refrigerate for 1 hour.

Remove the dough from the refrigerator, unwrap it, and place between 2 pieces of parchment paper. Roll out the dough into a rectangle about ⅛ inch thick. Remove the parchment paper, trim the rough edges of the dough, and transfer to the prepared baking sheet. Using a knife, cut the dough into 1-inch squares, circles, or desired shape, and spread them apart on the baking sheet. Brush each cracker with coconut oil and sprinkle with salt.

Bake for 12 minutes, and then rotate the baking sheet 180 degrees. Bake until crisp, 6 minutes. Let the crackers cool on the baking sheet for 5 minutes before serving.

makes 46 crackers

½ cup (70 GRAMS) **brown rice flour**

½ cup (50 GRAMS) **gluten-free oat flour**

⅓ cup (64 GRAMS) **potato starch**

¼ cup (33 GRAMS) **cornmeal**

2 tablespoons (28 GRAMS) **vegan sugar**

2 teaspoons **xanthan gum**

1 teaspoon **salt, plus more for sprinkling**

¼ cup (52 GRAMS) **melted unscented coconut oil, plus more for brushing**

1 tablespoon (22 GRAMS) **agave nectar**

⅓ cup (75 GRAMS) **cold water**

2½ cups (282 GRAMS) **grated vegan gluten-free cheese, or cheese of your choice**

butter crackers

This is the rarest of all BabyCakes recipes: Whereas all my other recipes are meant to be eaten almost immediately, these crackers actually hold up as the days go by. I happily ate them for three days after preparing a batch. Texturally they remind me of a Ritz cracker, and they're great crumbled into a salad or dipped into peanut butter and jelly, which is nowhere near as weird as you are making it out to be right now.

makes 55 crackers

½ cup (70 GRAMS) Bob's Red Mill Gluten-Free All-Purpose Baking Flour

¾ cup (105 GRAMS) brown rice flour

1 tablespoon (14 GRAMS) vegan sugar

1 teaspoon baking powder

½ teaspoon xanthan gum

2 teaspoons paprika

½ teaspoon salt, plus more for sprinkling

½ cup (112 GRAMS) Butter (page 133)

¼ cup (56 GRAMS) cold water

In a food processor, combine the flours, sugar, baking powder, xanthan gum, paprika, and salt and process for 15 seconds. Add the butter and pulse until the dough separates into small pebbles. Slowly pulse in the cold water just until a thick dough forms. Wrap the dough in plastic wrap and refrigerate for 1 hour.

Preheat the oven to 350°F. Line a baking sheet with parchment paper and set aside.

Remove the dough from the refrigerator, unwrap it, and place between 2 pieces of parchment paper. Roll out the dough into a large rectangle about ⅛ inch thick. Remove the parchment paper and cut out the crackers from the dough with a 1-inch round cookie cutter. Put them on the prepared baking sheet and sprinkle with salt.

Bake for 10 minutes, and then rotate the baking sheet 180 degrees. Bake until lightly golden, 5 minutes. Let the crackers cool on the baking sheet for 5 minutes before serving.

crispy banana and almond butter roll-up

serves 4

4 teaspoons (18 GRAMS) melted unscented coconut oil

3 bananas, sliced

¼ cup (104 GRAMS) almond butter

1 recipe (4 portions) Wrap Bread (page 50)

Pinch of ground cinnamon

Do not fret: Caramelizing bananas is one of the most gratifying experiences in the kitchen, mostly because it requires approximately no skill but makes it seem to the unversed outsider like you are some sort of culinary Rembrandt.

Heat the oil in a wide skillet set over medium heat. Add the bananas and cook until they are browned on the bottom, 2 minutes. Flip the bananas and cook until the second side is browned, about 1 more minute. Remove the pan from the heat and let cool for 5 minutes.

Spread the almond butter on each piece of wrap bread, top with the crispy bananas, and sprinkle with cinnamon. Fold ½ inch of one end over the filling, rotate 90 degrees, and roll it up into a cylinder. Serve these warm, please.

quesadillas

These are so easy you may come to rely on them a tad too often ("Quesadilla Wednesday!" becomes "Quesadilla October!" before you know it, trust me). The keys here are to find a vegan cheese your family prefers and to roll the tortillas out a bit thinner than you would for, say, a taco, so the quesadillas will crisp up nicely throughout.

2 teaspoons Butter (PAGE 133) or melted unscented coconut oil

4 Corn Tortillas (page 104)

2 cups (170 GRAMS) grated or shredded vegan gluten-free cheese (I prefer Daiya or Teese)

Heat ½ teaspoon of the butter in a wide skillet set over medium heat. Place a tortilla on the skillet and spread ½ cup of the cheese onto one half. Add 1 tablespoon water to the pan to create steam and cover the pan. Cook until the cheese is melted, 1 to 2 minutes. Fold the tortilla over to create a half-moon shape. Transfer the quesadilla to a cutting board. Repeat with the remaining ingredients.

Let the quesadillas cool for 2 minutes before cutting into quarters and serving.

butter and jelly bread

When I was young and grade school had let out, we were released into the kitchen to make snacks without supervision. Some days I took a stack of Oreos, other times a bowl of cereal. But when the ingredients permitted, my absolute go-to was a piece of Wonder Bread with soft butter and a modest helping of seedless strawberry jam (no lumps!). I would cut off the crusts and roll the thing into a sweet, buttery paradise. Now that I'm older and allowed to turn on the oven, I've created this, my favorite recipe in the entire book. (Well, it's in the top five, at least.)

serves 10

1 recipe dough for Wrap Bread (page 50)

½ cup (112 GRAMS) Butter (page 133), softened, or the nut spread of your choice

¾ cup (247 GRAMS) your favorite jam

Preheat the oven to 375°F.

Between 2 sheets of parchment paper, roll out the wrap bread dough into a 12 by 9-inch rectangle about ½ inch thick. Remove the top layer of parchment paper and place the long side of the dough toward you. Spread the butter over the entire surface of the dough, followed by a layer of jam on top. Starting at either of the two shorter sides, roll the dough up into a cylinder. Using the parchment to lift the roll, transfer it into a 9 by 4-inch loaf pan, parchment on the bottom. Trim the excess parchment paper.

Bake for 20 minutes, and then rotate the pan 180 degrees. Bake until the crust is golden and firm to the touch, 15 minutes. Let cool for 20 minutes before cutting.

potato and cauliflower tots

My daughter put herself on a strict carb-only diet on her first birthday, and to this day I need to hide spinach under pieces of potato and squish kale between tightly sealed pieces of bread to get her to eat it. For this recipe, I used cauliflower because it's white, and to be perfectly honest, that helps me stand a better chance of success. You should try this with broccoli if green still exists in your baby's color palette.

1 medium Idaho potato

1 head cauliflower, chopped

1½ tablespoons (15 GRAMS) chopped onion

2 tablespoons (28 GRAMS) melted unscented coconut oil or olive oil, plus more for brushing

½ cup (56 GRAMS) grated or shredded vegan gluten-free cheese (I prefer Daiya or Teese)

2 tablespoons (24 GRAMS) potato starch

Leaves from 2 sprigs rosemary

2 teaspoons salt

Preheat the oven to 350°F. Line 2 rimmed baking sheets with parchment paper and set aside.

Wrap the potato tightly in aluminum foil, poke thoroughly with a fork, and bake until a toothpick can be inserted easily, 1 hour.

In a medium bowl, combine the cauliflower, onions, and oil, and toss well. Spread the mixture out on one of the prepared baking sheets.

Bake for 30 minutes, and set aside.

Leaving the skin on, chop the potato into medium pieces and transfer to a food processor. Add the cauliflower mixture, vegan cheese, potato starch, rosemary, and salt, and pulse until the mixture looks like very lumpy mashed potatoes.

Brush the second prepared baking sheet lightly with oil. Using a tablespoon, scoop out some of the potato mixture, roll it into a cylinder shape, and put it on the baking sheet. Repeat with the remaining potato mixture. Brush each tot lightly with oil.

Bake for 8 minutes, and then rotate the baking sheet 180 degrees. Bake until golden and crisp, 8 minutes. Let the tots cool on the sheet for 10 minutes before serving.

raging party mix

It is baffling to me that I only recently thought to create a BabyCakes recipe for a party mix. Hopefully by the time you read this I will have coordinated the BabyCakes branches to be serving this at each of the registers. Because in the history of party mix, has there ever been a person who has successfully walked by a bowl without grabbing a handful or wanting to grab a handful? Exactly. (The answer is no.)

Preheat the oven to 250°F. Line a rimmed baking sheet with parchment paper and set aside.

In a large bowl, toss together the cereal, Oat Crackies, and the nuts, if using.

Heat the butter in a wide skillet set over medium heat. Add the Worcestershire sauce, salt, garlic powder, and the cayenne pepper, if using. Stir well, and then pour the mixture over the cereal mixture. Toss until well coated. Pour the mixture onto the prepared baking sheet.

Bake, stirring halfway through, until well toasted, 40 minutes. Let the mix cool on the baking sheet for 10 minutes before serving.

vegetables disguised

Stealthily adding steamed and/or pureed vegetables to kids' meals is nothing new, but by now you are aware that sometimes my recipes are delicate. What follows are a few helpful tips.

Green Bread: Steam and then puree one bunch of either spinach or Swiss chard (remove the stems first!). Press all of the excess water out of the vegetables as best as you're able, preferably using a sieve. Using a rubber spatula, fold the puree into the bread dough gently and bake as instructed. Do not exceed 2 cups vegetables per bread recipe. This works best with Sandwich Bread (page 47).

Kale Tortillas: After you prepare your dough for Corn Tortillas (page 104), place it in a food processor and pulse in 1 cup steamed kale. If the dough gets too loose, sprinkle in some corn flour to bind it up again. Proceed with the recipe as instructed.

Creamy White Sauce: Puree some steamed cauliflower, swirl it into the Béchamel Sauce (page 135), and use with your favorite pasta or pizza.

foreign affairs

By now our global supermarket has become an accessible, beautiful, but sometimes confusing place where just about everything is within finger's reach—if not at the local specialty store, then through thousands of online purveyors. For the bold and committed, the only limitation seems to be pantry space. Fortunately for this book and my eating tendencies, I have lots of storage space at BabyCakes NYC.

I was born in San Diego, California, about a millimeter from the Mexican border. That fine country's cuisine courses through my veins. Like sunburns, it is my birthright, and this chapter will reveal its many influences on how I approach cooking. But I now live in New York City, still and forever the greatest city in all the world. Here I've learned that there is more to life than cookies and guacamole (but not much more).

Like bread from Ethiopia! And scallion pancakes from China(town)! I've also included a flatbread that doubles as a naan, so when you're not in the mood for flour or corn tortillas (both in this chapter!), you will have some alternatives to keep you occupied. Ciao!

baked samosas with potato and green chile **SWEET CORN AND CILANTRO EMPANADAS** scallion pancakes **ZUCCHINI LATKES** flour tortillas **CORN TORTILLAS** flatbread **ETHIOPIAN BREAD**

baked samosas

with potato and green chile

From my Irish forebearers I inherited a delicate constitution. Maybe you and I share this weakness, owing to one food sensitivity or another. Fried food, more often than not, wreaks havoc on my stomach. So I bake my samosas, though these are also good fried.

Line 2 baking sheets with parchment paper and set aside.

Heat 1 tablespoon of the oil in a wide skillet set over medium heat. Add the garlic and cook, stirring occasionally, for 30 seconds. Add the green chiles, salt, coriander, and cumin and stir. Reduce the heat to medium-low, add the peas, and cook for 3 minutes. Gently add the potatoes, stir, and cook for 4 to 5 minutes. Stir in the garam masala and cook for 4 more minutes. Remove the pan from the heat and let the filling cool for 30 minutes.

Preheat the oven to 400°F.

Divide the pastry dough into golf ball–size portions. Roll each ball into a 6-inch-diameter circle, cut each circle in half, and brush water around the edges. In your hand, roll one piece of the dough into a cone shape and seal all the edges except the top. Spoon about 3 tablespoons of the samosa filling into the cone, pinch the top into a triangle shape to seal the edges, and put it on a prepared baking sheet. Repeat with the remaining ingredients. Brush the samosas with the remaining tablespoon of oil.

Bake for 12 minutes, and then rotate the sheets 180 degrees. Bake until golden, 6 minutes. Let the samosas cool on the baking sheets for 10 minutes before serving.

makes 14

2 tablespoons (28 GRAMS) melted unscented coconut oil

2 garlic cloves, minced

4 green chiles (canned will do), chopped

2 teaspoons salt

1 teaspoon ground coriander

½ teaspoon ground cumin

½ cup (75 GRAMS) green peas (frozen will do)

3 large Yukon Gold potatoes, boiled and cubed

¼ teaspoon garam masala

1 recipe All-Purpose Puff Pastry Dough (page 110)

sweet corn and cilantro empanadas

One of the biggest joys I found in developing a puff pastry was that it allowed me to explore new and mildly exotic (for me, anyway) uses for the dough. If you are one of those anti-cilantro folks, you can swap in any similar leafy herb and be just fine.

makes 16

2 tablespoons (28 GRAMS) melted unscented coconut oil, plus more for brushing

⅓ cup (50 GRAMS) chopped red onion

1¼ cups (170 GRAMS) frozen corn, thawed

2 garlic cloves, minced

¼ cup (56 GRAMS) coconut or rice milk

1 teaspoon white wine vinegar

¼ teaspoon cayenne pepper

1 teaspoon salt, plus more for sprinkling

2 tablespoons (1 GRAM) chopped fresh cilantro leaves

1 recipe All-Purpose Puff Pastry Dough (page 110)

Heat the oil in a wide skillet set over medium heat. Add the onion and cook, stirring occasionally, for 2 minutes. Add the corn, garlic, coconut milk, and vinegar and cook until the corn begins to brown slightly, 4 minutes. Add the cayenne pepper and salt, stir, and remove the pan from the heat.

Put three fourths of the corn mixture into a food processor and pulse until finely chopped. Return to the pan and fold in the cilantro.

Preheat the oven to 375°F. Line 2 baking sheets with parchment paper and set aside.

Between 2 pieces of parchment paper, roll out the pastry dough until it is about ¼ inch thick. Cut out the dough using a 4-inch round biscuit cutter, or a large rimmed glass about the same size. Place the pastry rounds on the prepared baking sheets. Scoop 1 tablespoon of filling in the center of each round, fold the pastry over to create a half-moon, and seal the edges with a fork. Brush the tops of the empanadas with oil and sprinkle with salt.

Bake for 12 minutes, and then rotate the sheets 180 degrees. Bake until they are golden, 6 minutes. Let the empanadas cool on the baking sheets for 10 minutes before serving.

scallion pancakes

If you are fortunate enough to live in an area with a bona fide Chinatown, you'll know these small pancakes as The Most Delicious Way to Live with Practically No Money. In the right cook's hands they are slight, with a bite of scallion and salt cutting through the sweet oil. I'll just assume you have Sriracha somewhere in the house. If not, take a minute to run and grab some now, before you begin this recipe.

In a large bowl, whisk together the flours, salt, and xanthan gum. Pour in the rice milk, hot water, and the 2 tablespoons oil and whisk until a pancake-like batter forms. Using a rubber spatula, fold in the scallions and garlic gently.

Heat about 2 tablespoons oil in a wide skillet set over medium heat. Scoop ⅓ cup of the batter into the pan and tilt the pan to spread the batter evenly. Cook until the top of the batter begins to bubble and dry slightly, 2 minutes. Flip the pancake and cook the second side until the bottom is browned, about 2 more minutes. Transfer to a plate. Repeat with the remaining batter until all the pancakes are cooked. Serve immediately.

makes 8

¾ cup (105 GRAMS) Bob's Red Mill Gluten-Free All-Purpose Baking Flour

¼ cup (25 GRAMS) gluten-free oat flour or brown rice flour

½ teaspoon salt

¼ teaspoon xanthan gum

½ cup (113 GRAMS) rice milk

½ cup (113 GRAMS) hot water

2 tablespoons (28 GRAMS) coconut oil, plus more for the skillet

3 scallions, chopped into ½-inch lengths

1 garlic clove, minced

zucchini latkes

Stovetop frying is an art form, the short-order cook at your local diner an artist of the highest calling. It took me a few dozen tries before I learned how to make them exactly the same each time, but it was a much-savored victory! (Pro tip: It's a difficult lesson, but try to avoid fussing with the pancake too much once it is in the pan.)

makes 6

2 medium zucchini, shredded

1 teaspoon salt

½ cup (70 GRAMS) Bob's Red Mill Gluten-Free All-Purpose Baking Flour

1 teaspoon baking powder

½ teaspoon xanthan gum

¼ teaspoon paprika

¼ cup (56 GRAMS) rice milk

1 scallion, thinly sliced

Freshly ground black pepper

3 tablespoons (42 GRAMS) melted unscented coconut oil

Preheat the oven to 375°F. Line a baking sheet with parchment paper and set aside.

In a medium bowl, combine the zucchini and the salt. Let sit for 20 minutes to extract some water.

In a separate medium bowl, whisk together the flour, baking powder, xanthan gum, and paprika. Add the rice milk and, using a rubber spatula, stir until a thick batter forms.

Drain the zucchini and, using 2 folded paper towels, press the zucchini firmly to remove any excess liquid. Add the drained zucchini to the batter and, using a rubber spatula, fold in the scallions. Season with pepper.

Heat 1 tablespoon of the oil in a wide skillet set over medium heat. Using a ¼-cup measuring cup, scoop 2 measures of the batter onto the pan. Cook the latkes until the bottom is browned, 2½ minutes. Flip the latkes and cook until the second side is browned, 2 minutes. Transfer to the prepared baking sheet. Repeat with the remaining batter.

Put the latkes in the oven and bake until crisp, 8 minutes. Let stand on the baking sheet for 3 minutes before serving.

flour tortillas

For whatever reason, a homemade tortilla remains a rare indulgence. Maybe this is because the store-bought varieties rank among the very few things that are believed to be entirely adequate. Maybe. But then you have a homemade tortilla and things are suddenly completely different. Tortillas are not mere vehicles for beans and vegetables and salsa (though that is a noble calling). Done right, they are almost dessert-like. They are small but weighty. When you place them in the pan they bloom poetically. Eaten warm, on their own, they offer a faint sweetness and a delicate texture that will have you questioning your entire Mexican food–eating history.

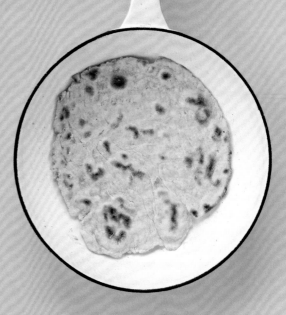

In a medium bowl, whisk together the flour, arrowroot, potato starch, sugar, salt, baking powder, and xanthan gum. Measure in the butter and work it in by hand, kneading gently. Add the milks and knead until a sticky dough forms. You may need to add a splash or two of water to get the dough wet enough so it binds together. Wrap the dough in plastic wrap and refrigerate for 1 hour.

Remove the dough from the refrigerator, unwrap it, and divide it into 12 equal-size balls. Roll each ball flat between 2 pieces of plastic wrap or parchment paper until each tortilla is about ⅛ inch thick (they puff up quite a bit, so do a test with one tortilla to determine how thick you prefer them).

Heat ½ teaspoon of the oil in a wide skillet set over medium heat. Put a tortilla into the skillet and cook until it starts to puff up, about 45 seconds. Flip the tortilla and cook until the second side is browned, 30 more seconds. Transfer the tortilla to a plate, cover with a dish towel, and repeat the process with the remaining tortillas and oil.

makes 12

1¼ cups (125 GRAMS) gluten-free oat flour

1 cup (120 GRAMS) arrowroot

¾ cup (144 GRAMS) potato starch

2 tablespoons (28 GRAMS) vegan sugar

2 teaspoons salt

1 teaspoon baking powder

1 teaspoon xanthan gum

3 tablespoons (42 GRAMS) Butter (page 133), softened

¾ cup (168 GRAMS) room-temperature rice milk

½ cup (113 GRAMS) room-temperature coconut milk

2 tablespoons (28 GRAMS) melted unscented coconut oil

corn tortillas

There's one strict rule here: You must use masa harina corn flour. (Our life-partner-in-baking, Bob's Red Mill, makes an outstanding version, which can be found in most reputable grocery stores.) Regular corn flour will not do, and neither will cornmeal. My version of these tortillas plays heavily on that salted corn flavor I love so much. If that bothers you, dropping the salt will not affect the outcome.

In a medium bowl, combine the masa harina, salt, and lukewarm water until a thick dough forms. If the dough is too dry, add 1 tablespoon warm water at a time until it comes together. Wrap the dough in plastic wrap and let it sit on the counter for 30 minutes.

Divide the dough into 6 equal-size balls. Between 2 pieces of plastic wrap or parchment paper, roll each ball flat until the tortilla is very thin, about ⅛ inch thick.

Heat ½ teaspoon of the oil in a wide skillet set over medium heat. Put a tortilla in the skillet and cook until it starts to puff up, about 45 seconds. Flip the tortilla and cook until the second side is browned, 30 more seconds. Transfer the cooked tortilla to a plate, cover with a dish towel, and repeat the process with the remaining tortillas and oil.

makes 6

- 2 cups (230 GRAMS) masa harina
- 1 teaspoon salt
- 1¼ cups (282 GRAMS) lukewarm water
- 1 tablespoon (14 GRAMS) melted unscented coconut oil

ideas for your tortillas

Here are two ideas for how to use your tortillas.

Chilaquiles: Quarter 6 Corn Tortillas (opposite) and set aside. Heat ¼ cup melted unscented coconut oil in a skillet set over medium-high heat. Add the tortilla pieces and cook until lightly golden, about 1 minute per side. Remove and drain on a paper towel. Pour 1 cup of your favorite salsa (enchilada sauce works well, too, as does anything in the Cholula family) into the same skillet and heat for 1 minute. Add the chips to the pan, mix them together with the sauce until each one is coated, and cook for 1 minute more. Transfer the chilaquiles to a plate, sprinkle a pinch of shredded vegan cheese on top, and serve hot.

Cinnamon-Sugar Chips: Preheat the oven to 325°F. Line a baking sheet with parchment paper and set aside. Place 6 Flour Tortillas (page 103) on a work surface; spread each with 1 tablespoon (14 grams) Butter (page 133), then sprinkle with 2 teaspoons vegan sugar and a pinch of cinnamon-sugar. Cut the tortillas into triangles and arrange them on the prepared baking sheet. Bake until crispy and golden brown, 10 to 12 minutes. Serve warm.

flatbread

This bread is soft and pillowy and versatile and gets so photogenically blistered in a hot pan that you'll have guests awestruck at your wizardry. I left the flavors open for you to explore, so you can mix and match with whichever herbs and spices you prefer. I've often seen restaurants brush it with olive oil and toss it in an oregano mixture, and it works well—just do that before you begin cooking it. Or! Do you like naan? If you add two teaspoons baking soda with your dry ingredients, you will have naan.

makes 8

½ cup (70 GRAMS) Bob's Red Mill Gluten-Free All-Purpose Baking Flour

¾ cup (75 GRAMS) gluten-free oat flour

½ cup (60 GRAMS) arrowroot

2 tablespoons (28 GRAMS) vegan sugar

2 teaspoons salt

1 teaspoon xanthan gum

½ teaspoon baking powder

½ cup (120 GRAMS) coconut milk

2 tablespoons (28 GRAMS) melted unscented coconut oil, plus more for the skillet

In a medium bowl, whisk together the flours, arrowroot, sugar, salt, xanthan gum, and baking powder. Pour in the coconut milk and the 2 tablespoons oil and, using a rubber spatula, stir until a thick dough forms. If the dough is too dry, add water one splash at a time.

Scoop a heaping golf ball–size portion of dough onto a sheet of plastic wrap. Place another sheet of plastic wrap over the top and roll the dough into a rectangle about ¼ inch thick. Repeat with the remaining dough.

Heat about 1 teaspoon oil in a wide skillet set over medium heat. Put the dough into the skillet and cook until the bottom is browned and bubbles form on the top, 1½ minutes. Flip it over and cook for 2 more minutes. Transfer the bread to a plate. Repeat the process until all of the dough is cooked, preparing one at a time.

Serve warm.

ethiopian bread

Before I created this recipe, I was a complete amateur with teff flour. I've learned that it is fairly delicate compared with the other flours I use, but the flavor is outstanding. If you allow the dough to sit overnight (at least), it will ferment into a completely unique tangy tartness, almost like a sourdough. If your bread is coming out too crisp, add a quarter cup of flour to give it some volume.

In a medium bowl, whisk together the teff flour and water. Cover with a dish towel and let it sit on the countertop for at least 24 hours. The next day, stir in the ground flaxseed, baking soda, and salt.

Heat 1 teaspoon of the oil in a wide skillet set over medium heat. Scoop ⅓ cup of the batter into the pan and tilt the pan to spread the batter evenly. Cook until the top of the batter begins to bubble and dry slightly, 1 minute. Flip the bread and cook the second side about 1 more minute. Transfer to a plate. Repeat with the remaining batter and oil as needed until all the bread is cooked. Serve immediately.

makes 8

1½ cups (180 GRAMS) **teff flour**

2 cups (452 GRAMS) **water**

2 tablespoons (14 GRAMS) **ground flaxseed (flax meal)**

⅛ teaspoon **baking soda**

¾ teaspoon **salt**

1 tablespoon (14 GRAMS) **melted unscented coconut oil**

puff pastry and beyond

As you know, puff pastry has thousands of absolutely beautiful uses, both savory and sweet, from tarts to pot pies; almost all great cuisines have many uses for it. The recipes that follow utilize vegetables left in their savory states, even if deep in their hearts some may want to be desserts.

Much like the BabyCakes pie dough, the puff pastry I make is fairly forgiving (more than we can say for yours, France!). You can rip off the ends if they're hanging over weirdly, or else break off a piece here to fill in a patch there. It may turn out that these mistakes are your favorite part of the final dish: Puff-pastry patchwork creates the occasional crunchy knuckle of crust that everyone loves to nibble on so much.

all-purpose puff pastry dough VEGETABLE POT PIE
potato and leek tart ONION AND CURED BLACK OLIVE TART
fennel, spinach, and leek crostata MUSHROOM TURNOVERS

all-purpose puff pastry dough

I gained seven pounds in pursuit of this recipe. I don't regret it. (Though I'm thankful to have solved its riddle before my pants situation got seriously out of control.)

makes 1¹/₄ pounds

2 cups (280 GRAMS) Bob's Red Mill Gluten-Free All-Purpose Baking Flour

½ cup (50 GRAMS) gluten-free oat flour

1¼ cups (150 GRAMS) arrowroot

⅓ cup (70 GRAMS) vegan sugar

2 teaspoons salt

2¼ teaspoons active dry yeast

2 teaspoons xanthan gum

1 teaspoon baking powder

1¾ cups (420 GRAMS) room-temperature coconut milk

½ cup (112 GRAMS) melted unscented coconut oil

1 cup plus 2 tablespoons (252 GRAMS) chilled Butter (page 133)

In a medium bowl, whisk together the flours, arrowroot, sugar, salt, yeast, xanthan gum, and baking powder. Pour in the coconut milk and oil and, using a rubber spatula, stir until a thick dough forms. If the dough is too dry, add lukewarm water 1 tablespoon at a time. Wrap the dough in plastic and refrigerate for 2 hours.

Put the dough and the butter into a food processor and pulse until the dough is freckled with quarter-size pieces of butter. Wrap the dough in plastic and refrigerate for 1 more hour.

Between 2 pieces of parchment paper, roll out the dough into the desired shape.

Bake in a preheated 375°F oven (the amount of time will change based on the filling).

there is no such thing as extra puff pastry dough

Obviously I am taking issue with the word *extra*. Can you have "extra" pastry dough? If it's not the exact perfect amount, it isn't enough! So let's rephrase: I intentionally created the recipes for Croissants (page 30) and for All-Purpose Puff Pastry Dough (opposite) to leave you with some "bonus" dough to store in the freezer. Here are some things you could try as your frozen collection amasses over time.

Salted Chocolate Tartlets: Mold the pastry dough into the pan of your choosing (mini muffin pan, maybe?). Bake in a 350°F preheated oven for 20 minutes. Let cool. Over a double boiler, melt 2 cups (480 grams) vegan semisweet chocolate chips and slowly swirl in ⅓ cup (75 grams) coconut milk. Pour the chocolate mixture into the pastry shells, top with coarse salt, and let the tartlets harden for 1 hour before serving.

Apple Strudel: Chop 3 apples of any variety into ¼-inch cubes and toss with sugar, agave nectar, or coconut sugar and a dash of cinnamon. Mold the pastry dough into

a baking dish and add the apple mixture. Bake in a 350°F preheated oven for 25 to 30 minutes and let cool for 30 minutes before serving.

Pop Tarts: Roll the dough out into a 16-inch rectangle and trim the edges. Cut the rectangle into 3 × 4-inch rectangles. Fill half of the rectangles with 1 tablespoon each of your preferred jam, leaving a ½-inch border. Brush the edges with agave nectar, and then place a second rectangle on top. Using a fork, seal the edges. Bake in a 350°F preheated oven for 15 minutes. Let cool on the baking sheet for 5 minutes, and serve.

vegetable pot pie

This thing is, like, the anti-cupcake. Big and hearty—macho, even. Maybe you have your own ideas for how to fill the pie; I can dig that. As long as the crust is done right and your filling ingredients aren't massively out of proportion, you can really tinker to your heart's content and it will taste great.

serves 6

¼ cup (56 GRAMS) melted Butter (page 133), plus more for brushing the baking dish

1 cup (150 GRAMS) cubed potatoes

½ small yellow onion, chopped

½ cup (64 GRAMS) cubed carrots

1 celery stalk, chopped

2 garlic cloves, minced

½ cup (82 GRAMS) fresh corn or thawed frozen corn

2 tablespoons (15 GRAMS) arrowroot

1 cup (88 GRAMS) broccoli florets

1 cup (100 GRAMS) cauliflower florets

1 cup (67 GRAMS) roughly chopped stemmed kale

Salt and freshly ground black pepper

½ recipe All-Purpose Puff Pastry Dough (page 110)

2 tablespoons chopped fresh sage leaves

Leaves from 1 sprig rosemary

¼ teaspoon ground nutmeg

Heat 2 tablespoons of the butter in a wide skillet set over medium heat. Add the potatoes, onion, carrots, celery, and garlic and cook until lightly browned, about 10 minutes, stirring occasionally. Add the corn and arrowroot and cook for 3 more minutes.

In a large pot, bring 2 quarts water to a boil. Add the broccoli, cauliflower, and kale. Reduce the heat to low and simmer the vegetables until they soften, 8 minutes. Drain the vegetables, transfer them to a large bowl, and press out any excess water with paper towels. Add the potato mixture to the bowl and then add the sage, rosemary, nutmeg, and salt and pepper to taste. Using a rubber spatula, stir together gently and allow to cool for 15 minutes.

Preheat the oven to 375°F. Brush a baking dish with butter.

Roll out the chilled pastry between 2 sheets of parchment into a 12½ by 9-inch rectangle, about ⅛ inch thick. Remove the parchment paper and mold the pastry to fit the shape of the baking dish. Pour the vegetable mixture into the baking dish and cover with the pastry dough. Using a paring knife, score the top of the dough in 4 or 5 places. Brush the top with the remaining 2 tablespoons butter.

Bake for 15 minutes, and then rotate the baking dish 180 degrees. Bake until golden and bubbling, 10 minutes. Let the pot pie cool for 10 minutes before serving.

potato and leek tart

Potato and leek is one of the truly great flavor combinations in cooking. Until now I haven't had much cause to use it. I sometimes use this recipe to make tartlets because (a) they are cute and (b) I tend to snack compulsively, but it's really most practical as one big happy tart, whether for dinner or brunch.

Heat the oil in a wide skillet set over medium heat. Add the leeks, salt, and pepper to taste. Cook, stirring occasionally, until the leeks are slightly browned, 5 minutes. Fold in the potatoes and cook for 7 minutes or until the potatoes are golden brown. Sprinkle in the rosemary and remove from the heat and allow to cool for 15 minutes.

Preheat the oven to 375°F. Line a baking sheet with parchment paper and set a 9-inch tart mold on top.

Between 2 pieces of parchment paper, roll out the chilled dough into a circle ¼ inch thick. Remove the parchment paper, transfer the dough to the tart pan, and softly push it into the mold. Cut off the excess dough that hangs over the side and save for another use. Pour the potato-leek mixture into the tart and spread evenly.

Bake for 15 minutes, and then rotate the sheet 180 degrees. Bake until the potatoes are soft and the crust is golden brown, 10 minutes. Let the tart cool for 15 minutes before serving.

serves 8

1 tablespoon (14 GRAMS) melted unscented coconut oil

2 leeks (light green and white parts only), thinly sliced

1 teaspoon salt

Freshly cracked black pepper

2 red potatoes, chopped

Leaves from 2 sprigs rosemary

½ recipe All-Purpose Puff Pastry Dough (page 110), or ½ recipe dough for Croissants (page 30) or Spelt Croissants (page 32)

onion and cured black olive tart

I beg you: To preserve the dignity of this classic tart, please refrain from using canned olives. The hope is that somewhere on your shopping route, there is a place for cured black olives, the kind that are available in bulk at most large-scale markets by now. This is my version of the time-tested onion-and-olive combo. I'm not super crazy about a *billion* caramelized onions, so I use a bit less than do other chefs and bakers, relying on the crust to carry the day. You are fine to bump it up on the onion front because the pastry dough can handle as many as two large onions.

3 tablespoons (42 GRAMS) melted unscented coconut oil

1½ medium onions, thinly sliced

2 tablespoons (1 GRAM) fresh thyme leaves

½ recipe All-Purpose Puff Pastry Dough (page 110), or ½ recipe dough for Croissants (page 30) or Spelt Croissants (page 32)

¼ cup (30 GRAMS) halved and pitted cured black olives

Salt and freshly ground black pepper

Preheat the oven to 375°F. Line a baking sheet with parchment paper, place a 9-inch tart mold on top, and set aside.

Heat 1 tablespoon of the oil in a wide skillet set over medium heat. Add the onions and cook, stirring occasionally, until tender, about 3 minutes. Add the thyme and remove from the heat.

Between 2 pieces of parchment paper, roll out the dough into a circle ¼ inch thick. Remove the parchment paper, transfer the dough to the tart pan, and softly push it into the mold. Cut off the excess dough that hangs over the side and save for another use. Brush the dough with the remaining 2 tablespoons oil. Spoon the onion mixture into the dough, top with the olives, and season with salt and pepper.

Bake until golden brown, 20 to 25 minutes. Let the tart cool for 10 minutes before serving.

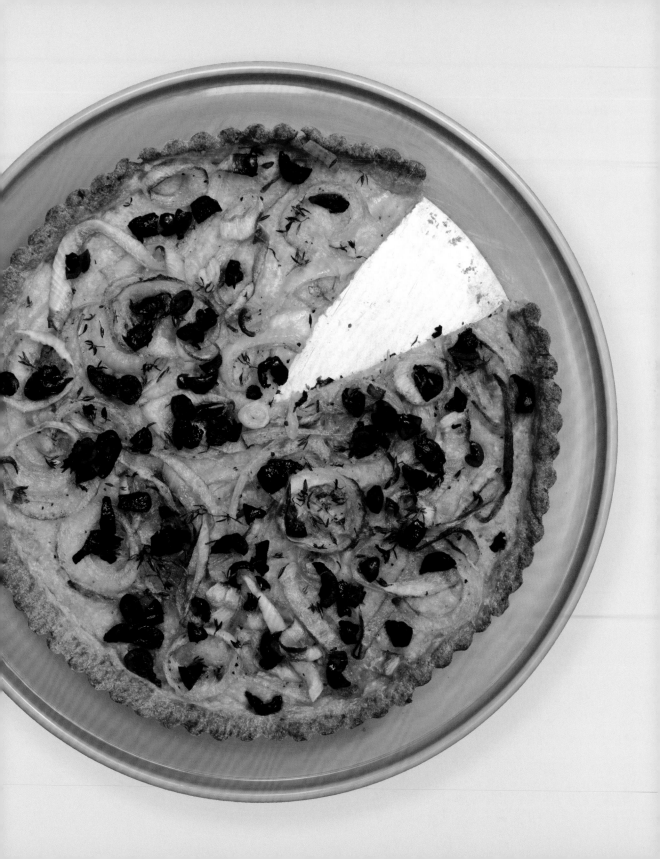

fennel, spinach, and leek crostata

I learned how to make a traditional crostata from my friend Brooks Headley, the James Beard Award–winning executive pastry chef of Del Posto in New York City. He taught me how important it is to remember to keep it simple and how it's pretty lame to be overly prissy anyway. He showed me, an Irish girl from California, how to channel my inner Italian *nonna*. And it worked! Be confident, intuitive. You can't mess this recipe up unless you undercook your vegetables, so don't do that.

¼ cup (56 GRAMS) olive oil

1 large fennel bulb, cored and roughly chopped

2 large leeks (light green and white parts only), thinly sliced

1 garlic clove, minced

4 cups (120 GRAMS) baby spinach

Salt and freshly ground black pepper

1 recipe All-Purpose Puff Pastry Dough (page 110)

1 tablespoon (.5 GRAM) fresh thyme leaves

1 tablespoon (1 GRAM) chopped fresh sage leaves

Line a baking sheet with parchment paper and set aside.

Heat 2 tablespoons of the olive oil in a wide skillet set over medium heat. Add the fennel and leeks and cook, stirring occasionally, until soft, about 4 minutes. Add the garlic and cook for 1 minute. Add the spinach and cook until wilted, about 1 minute. Season with salt and pepper to taste and drizzle with the remaining 2 tablespoons olive oil. Allow to cool for 15 minutes.

Preheat the oven to 400°F.

Between 2 pieces of parchment paper, roll out the chilled dough into a thin circle about ½ inch thick. Remove the parchment paper and transfer the dough to the prepared baking sheet. Pour the vegetables into the center of the dough and spread out to cover the surface, leaving a ¾-inch border. Starting at the top and moving clockwise, fold the edges of the dough toward the center over the vegetables. It doesn't have to be neat. Sprinkle the thyme and sage on top.

Bake for 15 minutes, and then rotate the baking sheet 180 degrees. Bake until the crust is golden, 10 minutes. Let the crostata cool on the baking sheet for 15 minutes before serving.

mushroom turnovers

Mushrooms have long been a vegan's best friend. They're substantial, versatile, and extremely receptive to just about any seasoning and method of preparation. I tried this recipe with a variety of mushrooms—everything from portobello to shiitake—and got excellent results each time.

makes 24

¼ cup (56 GRAMS) olive oil

½ medium onion, chopped

1¼ pounds (566 GRAMS) button mushrooms, trimmed and thinly sliced

Salt and freshly ground black pepper

Leaves from 2 sprigs rosemary

½ tablespoon chopped fresh sage

½ recipe All-Purpose Puff Pastry Dough (page 110), or ½ recipe dough for Croissants (page 30) or Spelt Croissants (page 32)

Preheat the oven to 400°F. Line a baking sheet with parchment paper and set aside.

Heat 2 tablespoons of the oil in a wide skillet set over medium heat. Add the onion and cook, stirring occasionally, until golden brown, about 4 minutes. Add the mushrooms and cook until the mushrooms are tender, about 4 minutes. Season with salt and pepper, toss in the herbs, drizzle with the remaining 2 tablespoons olive oil, stir, and set aside and allow to cool for 15 minutes

Between 2 pieces of parchment paper, roll out the chilled dough until it is about ¼ inch thick. Remove the parchment paper and, using a 3-inch round biscuit cutter, cut out the dough into circles. Put 1 tablespoon of the mushroom mixture onto half of each circle, leaving a ¼-inch border. Fold the pastry over to create a half-moon and seal the edges with a fork to create a ruffled look. Put the turnovers on the prepared baking sheet.

Bake for 8 minutes, and then rotate the baking sheet 180 degrees. Bake until golden, 8 minutes. Let the turnovers cool on the baking sheet for 10 minutes before serving.

snacks

At its absolute best, a snack will be in perfect harmony with the occasion. In my mind, there are so many varieties: purse snacks, park snacks, after-school snacks, midnight snacks, waiting-for-the-train snacks, and work snacks. Describing snacks stresses me out because they are such an important part of my life and I want so badly to do them justice.

I've preferred snacks to meals for as long as I can remember. This is in part because I hate feeling overstuffed, and snacks provide just enough energy to get by for the immediate future—until it's time for the next snack. I guess really it's just a way for me to eat more things.

I've actually developed a snacking strategy for you. The Oat Crackies (page 122) go in your purse, briefcase, toddler snack bag, or tote, as they are odorless and easy to sneak, and satisfy both salty and sweet cravings. The Almond-Rosemary Crackers (page 127) should be kept in plastic containers in various parts of your house or apartment (don't forget the baby's room!) for easy access. Take the Kale Chips (page 126) with you in a plastic bag to eat after your workout, but no earlier than ten in the morning. These guidelines work for me and I think they will work for you, too.

oat crackies **BREADSTICKS** pretzels **KALE CHIPS**
almond-rosemary crackers

oat crackies

In many circles, Wheat Thins are considered the greatest of all crackers. In my house I've witnessed entire boxes evaporate over the course of an hour. My oat version, named "Crackies" because that's what our daughter calls them, is built around what I remember as the best part of this munchie: salt. I replicated wheat, using oat flour and flax meal instead, and then added a spot of cornmeal for crunch, followed by a little sugar to bring it all together.

In a medium bowl, whisk together the oat flour, potato starch, cornmeal, ground flaxseed, sugar, xanthan gum, and salt. Add the oil, cold water, vanilla, and agave nectar and, using a rubber spatula, stir until a thick dough forms. If the dough is too dry, add more water 1 tablespoon at a time. Wrap the dough with plastic wrap and refrigerate for 1 hour.

Preheat the oven to 300°F. Line a baking sheet with parchment paper and set aside.

Remove the dough from the refrigerator, unwrap it, and place between 2 pieces of parchment paper. Roll out the dough until it is about 1/8 inch thick. Remove the parchment paper, trim off the rough edges of the dough, and cut it into 2-inch squares. Put the squares onto the prepared baking sheet, brush with oil, and sprinkle lightly with salt.

Bake for 15 minutes, and then rotate the baking sheet 180 degrees. Bake until lightly browned, 6 minutes. Let the crackers cool on the baking sheet for 5 minutes before serving.

makes 42

1 cup (100 GRAMS) **gluten-free oat flour**

1/3 cup plus 1 tablespoon (72 GRAMS) **potato starch**

1/4 cup (33 GRAMS) **cornmeal**

2 tablespoons (14 GRAMS) **ground flaxseed (flax meal)**

2 tablespoons (28 GRAMS) **vegan sugar**

2 teaspoons **xanthan gum**

1 teaspoon **salt, plus more for sprinkling**

1/4 cup (56 GRAMS) **melted unscented coconut oil, plus more for brushing**

1/4 cup (56 GRAMS) **cold water**

2 teaspoons **pure vanilla extract**

1 tablespoon (22 GRAMS) **agave nectar**

breadsticks

These came about quite by accident as I was fooling around with a messed-up batch of dough while talking on the phone. What I ended up creating was the best breadstick I have eaten since I was introduced to them at Pizza Hut in fifth grade while celebrating my best friend Clarissa's birthday. Clarissa, you won't believe it!

Line a rimmed baking sheet with parchment paper and set aside.

In a large bowl, whisk together the rice flour, oat flour, potato starch, arrowroot, sugar, salt, xanthan gum, baking powder, and yeast. Add the lukewarm milks and, with a rubber spatula, mix until the dough pulls away easily from the sides of the bowl. Add 1 tablespoon arrowroot at a time if the batter is not pulling away. Add a splash of lukewarm water if the dough is too dry.

Wrap the dough in plastic wrap and place in the refrigerator for 1 hour.

Remove the dough from the refrigerator, unwrap it, and portion out 24 small balls. Lightly dust your countertop with rice flour, roll each ball into a 6-inch rope, and then transfer to the baking sheet. Once all the breadsticks are formed, cover with a dish towel and allow to rise for 1 hour.

Preheat the oven to 400°F.

Bake the breadsticks for 6 minutes, rotate the sheet 180 degrees, and continue baking for another 3 minutes, or until the crust is golden brown. Remove the breadsticks from the oven and let them cool for 5 minutes before serving.

makes 24

- 1¼ cups (175 GRAMS) brown rice flour, plus more for rolling the dough
- ½ cup (50 GRAMS) gluten-free oat flour
- 1⅓ cups (256 GRAMS) potato starch
- 1 cup (120 GRAMS) arrowroot, or more if needed
- 2 tablespoons (28 GRAMS) vegan sugar
- 1 tablespoon (15 GRAMS) salt
- 1 teaspoon xanthan gum
- 1 tablespoon (15 GRAMS) baking powder
- 2¼ teaspoons active dry yeast
- ½ cup (120 GRAMS) lukewarm coconut milk
- 1 cup (226 GRAMS) lukewarm rice milk

pretzels

There are recipes that are esteem builders, and this is definitely one of them. Pretzels are not exactly simple to make, but once you get a handle on the technique, you will look deep into the eyes of other pretzel makers and find unspoken camaraderie. Here's a good tip to help get you there: If you are nervous about your pretzels losing shape when they hit the boiling water (totally a fair concern!), freeze the dough for a few hours after it is formed and they'll hold up better during the boil.

1 cup (226 GRAMS) warm water (about 120°F)

¼ cup (56 GRAMS) vegan sugar

2¼ teaspoons active dry yeast

1¾ cups (245 GRAMS) brown rice flour

1 cup (140 GRAMS) Bob's Red Mill Gluten-Free All-Purpose Baking Flour

2 tablespoons (28 GRAMS) melted unscented coconut oil, plus more for brushing the baking sheet

1 tablespoon (17 GRAMS) baking powder

1 teaspoon xanthan gum

1 teaspoon salt

3 tablespoons (45 GRAMS) baking soda

In a small bowl, combine the warm water, sugar, and yeast. Stir once and set aside to proof until it bubbles, about 10 minutes.

In a medium bowl, whisk together the flours, oil, baking powder, xanthan gum, and salt. Add the yeast mixture and, using a rubber spatula, stir until a thick, sticky dough forms. Cover the dough with a dish towel and let it sit on the countertop for 1 hour. Wrap the dough in plastic wrap and set aside.

Line a baking sheet with parchment paper, brush lightly with oil, and set it aside.

Portion the dough into balls the size of Ping-Pong balls. Using your hands, roll each portion into a rope about 6 inches in length. Twist each rope into a pretzel shape, pressing the ends tightly together so they hold their shape. Put them on the prepared baking sheet.

Preheat the oven to 400°F.

In a large pot, bring 3 inches of water to a boil over high heat and add the baking soda. Reduce the heat so the water just simmers. Put 1 pretzel in the water and boil for 45 seconds. Using tongs, turn it over and cook the second side for 30 seconds. Transfer the pretzel to a wire rack to drain. Repeat with the remaining pretzels. Once the pretzels are completely drained, return them to the baking sheet, leaving 1 inch between them.

Bake for 5 minutes, and then rotate the baking sheet 180 degrees. Bake until browned, 5 minutes. Let the pretzels cool on the baking sheet for 10 minutes before serving.

making your pretzels with spelt

There are reasons you might want to do pretzels with spelt. For one, spelt is cheaper. Also they come out a bit lighter, they involve fewer ingredients, and in general they are a bit simpler because spelt is easier to work with. To convert my recipe to spelt (it's so easy!), swap out the original list of ingredients in the recipe with the following list of ingredients and measurements, and proceed with the exact same baking instructions. Yes!

1 cup (226 GRAMS) **warm water (about 120°F)**

1 tablespoon (22 GRAMS) **agave nectar**

2¼ teaspoons **active dry yeast**

2¾ cups (385 GRAMS) **white spelt flour**

2 tablespoons (28 GRAMS) **melted unscented coconut oil, plus more for brushing the baking sheet**

1 tablespoon **salt** (18 GRAMS)

kale chips

I'm completely unsure why, but these chips are the most divisive snack on the planet. You either like them or they make you hostile. My monthly budget for kale chips, before this recipe, was . . . I don't even want to say. It was a lot, let's leave it at that. Little did I know the recipe was well within reach and in the process I could save enough money to invest in a totally new side snack!

1 bunch kale, stemmed

2 tablespoons (28 GRAMS) melted unscented coconut oil

⅓ cup (40 GRAMS) sesame seeds

¼ cup (30 GRAMS) nutritional yeast

1 teaspoon salt

¼ teaspoon cayenne pepper

Preheat the oven to 250°F. Line 2 baking sheets with parchment paper and set aside.

Put the kale in a bowl and add the oil, sesame seeds, nutritional yeast, salt, and cayenne pepper. Using your hands, toss until each leaf is well coated. Transfer the kale to the prepared baking sheets.

Bake, stirring halfway through, until crispy, about 30 minutes. Let the kale chips cool on the baking sheets for 5 minutes before serving.

almond-rosemary crackers

I avoid almond flour at the bakery because I'm sensitive to the plight of those with nut allergies, but it's necessary for this recipe. Almond flour provides a perfectly faint hint of sweetness. If you must replace the almond flour, try experimenting with rice flour.

makes 36 crackers

- 1½ cups (168 GRAMS) blanched almond flour
- ½ cup (50 GRAMS) gluten-free oat flour
- ⅓ cup (64 GRAMS) potato starch
- 2 tablespoons (2 GRAMS) chopped fresh rosemary leaves
- 1 teaspoon xanthan gum
- 1 teaspoon salt
- 2 tablespoons (28 GRAMS) melted unscented coconut oil
- ½ cup (113 GRAMS) cold water

Preheat the oven to 350°F. Line a baking sheet with parchment paper and set aside.

In a medium bowl, whisk together the flours, potato starch, rosemary, xanthan gum, and salt. Pour in the coconut oil and cold water and, using a rubber spatula, stir until a thick dough forms. Wrap the dough in plastic wrap and refrigerate for 1 hour.

Remove the dough from the refrigerator, unwrap it, and place it between 2 pieces of parchment paper. Roll out the dough into a large 16 by 12-inch rectangle about ⅛ inch thick. Remove the parchment paper, trim off the edges of the dough, and transfer it to the prepared baking sheet. Using a knife, cut the dough into 2½-inch rectangles.

Bake for 10 minutes, and then rotate the baking sheet 180 degrees. Bake until lightly golden, 5 minutes. Let the crackers cool on the baking sheet for 10 minutes before serving.

dips and dressings, a sauce, a spread, and butter

Basically: condiments. But what a lousy word, right? It fails to convey much of anything, if you ask me, so I chose to name this chapter a tad more literally. Because I love this chapter with all my being.

Let's just talk about butter for a minute, can we? You have in your hands a baking book, and perhaps that is owing to the fact that you've come across the name BabyCakes in the past. Definitely by now you have at least an idea of what we do and don't do there. Did you expect a butter recipe? Neither did I! Yet here it is. For me it was life-changing, and I think it may be for you, too. Learn it quick: My butter recipe is a part of this book's DNA.

And what lovely company it keeps in the pages ahead . . . it's all here! Let's get to it.

caesar dressing MAYONNAISE kale artichoke dip
BUTTER hummus BÉCHAMEL SAUCE

caesar dressing

A girl cannot live on vinaigrette alone, and I wouldn't offend you by assuming you are without your own faithful oil-and-vinegar concoction already. Instead I'm including this lo-fi Caesar, in part because it is perfect to use as a segue into your own renditions of all kinds of cream-based dressings. As you begin to swap out or add new herbs and ingredients to your liking, you'll quickly discover that even the slightest modification makes all the difference. Your first stop should be using this recipe on the salad you place on top of the Pizza with a Salad on Top (page 76).

(page 76)

makes 1 cup

- **4 tablespoons** (56 GRAMS) **Mayonnaise (opposite)**
- **2 teaspoons spicy mustard**
- **2 garlic cloves**
- **1 teaspoon salt**
- **⅔ cup** (140 GRAMS) **olive oil**
- **1 tablespoon plus 1 teaspoon** (20 GRAMS) **fresh lemon juice**
- **Freshly cracked black pepper**

In a blender, combine the mayonnaise, mustard, garlic, and salt and pulse until the garlic is minced. With the blender running on a medium setting, add the olive oil and lemon juice and blend for 30 seconds. Pour the dressing in a bowl and season with pepper. The dressing will keep in an airtight container in the refrigerator for 7 days.

mayonnaise

I eat a lot of Vegenaise, and I feel just okay about it. It has a great flavor and brings necessary moisture to ingredients that, as we all know, can lead to dry meals. But in the end, I got sick of paying for it, so I created my own. I think you're really going to like this and find a lot of uses for it! You can use your imagination, but turning it into salad dressing is one really simple and obvious way. I often do a number on it for Caesar Dressing (opposite).

In a food processor, combine the rice milk, vinegar, agave nectar, lecithin, salt, and dry mustard, and blend well. With the processor running, slowly add 1 cup of the oil and 1 tablespoon of the lemon juice. Then add the remaining 1¼ cups oil and the remaining ½ tablespoon lemon juice. Taste and adjust the seasoning. Pour the mayonnaise into an airtight container and chill for 2 hours before serving. The mayonnaise will keep in an airtight container in the refrigerator for 7 days.

makes 3¼ cups

¾ cup (170 GRAMS) rice milk

½ teaspoon apple cider vinegar

½ teaspoon agave nectar

2 teaspoons sunflower lecithin granules

1½ teaspoons salt

¼ teaspoon dry mustard

2¼ cups (540 GRAMS) olive oil

1½ tablespoons (22.5 GRAMS) fresh lemon juice

kale artichoke dip

It's all fun and games as everyone forks away spastically at a dish of sizzling, gooey artichoke dip. But then, as it quickly cools, the fat congeals inside the dish for all to see. The grease shimmers, and in it the reflections of six concerned souls. Shame rears its hideous face. "What did I even just eat?" "I didn't have too much, right?" "Is there a gym nearby?" "Will I have a heart attack tonight in my sleep?" My intention here is to show you that it is unnecessary to dose artichoke dip with ladles full of mayo and monstrous globules of cheese. This recipe may not help you lose weight, but it's also not going to fast-track you to the ER. If you feel very strongly about honoring this recipe's legacy of overwhelming creaminess, I can respect that: Add three tablespoons of the Mayonnaise (page 131) and you'll get there quick. Serve this with very simple bread or unsalted crackers to offset the caloric intensity!

serves 6

2 tablespoons (28 GRAMS) melted unscented coconut oil or olive oil

¼ small yellow onion, chopped

2 cups (135 GRAMS) kale, stemmed and roughly chopped

4 scallions, thinly sliced

1 garlic clove, minced

1 (12-OUNCE; 340-GRAM) bag frozen artichokes (or canned if you absolutely must), thawed

¼ cup (28 GRAMS) shredded vegan gluten-free cheese (optional)

1 tablespoon (15 GRAMS) fresh lemon juice

2 tablespoons (28 GRAMS) coconut milk

2 teaspoons (10 GRAMS) salt

¼ teaspoon (1 GRAM) ground nutmeg

Freshly ground black pepper

Preheat the oven to 350°F.

Heat the oil in a wide skillet set over medium heat. Add the onion and cook until tender, about 3 minutes. Add the kale, scallions, and garlic, and cook until the kale softens, about 5 minutes. Remove the pan from the heat and let cool for 20 minutes.

Transfer the kale mixture to a food processor and add the artichokes, vegan cheese (if using), lemon juice, coconut milk, salt, and nutmeg, and season with pepper. Pulse the mixture until it is semi-smooth. Pour the mixture into a baking dish.

Bake until the top is golden brown, 30 minutes. Let the dip cool for 5 to 10 minutes before serving.

butter

I've always thought that the BabyCakes frosting tasted faintly like a sweet butter, but I was never so delusional as to think I could cook savory recipes with it. To manipulate it from its happy state as a cake-topper, I first omitted the agave nectar, hoping it would take us somewhere joyful. It was atrocious. So I decided to switch out the emulsifier, which was when I discovered sunflower lecithin (conveniently soy-free!). It took a long while after that to perfect it, but I eventually lowered the eyebrows of even my most butter-loving Francophile pals. At the bakery, we use a regular loaf pan to set the butter, but feel free to use any mold you like.

makes 3½ cups

1½ cups (336 GRAMS) melted unscented coconut oil

1 cup (224 GRAMS) canola oil

¾ cup (224 GRAMS) rice milk

¼ cup (56 GRAMS) coconut milk

1 teaspoon agave nectar

2 tablespoons (18 GRAMS) granular sunflower lecithin

1 tablespoon (18 GRAMS) salt

2 teaspoons xanthan gum

1 tablespoon (15 GRAMS) fresh lemon juice

Line a shallow pan, such as a loaf pan, with parchment paper and set aside.

In a liquid measuring cup, combine the coconut oil and canola oil, stir gently, and set aside.

In a blender or food processor, combine the rice milk, coconut milk, agave nectar, sunflower lecithin, salt, and xanthan gum and blend for 1 minute. Very slowly add half of the oil mixture, followed by the lemon juice, and then the remaining oil mixture. Blend for 1 more minute.

Pour the mixture into the prepared pan and refrigerate until solid, about 3½ hours. Chop the butter into 1-inch cubes and store in an airtight container for up to 7 days.

hummus

I'll go out on a limb and say hummus is the most universally loved food to have come to America in the last couple of decades. I know it has been here longer, living a glorious existence among the hippies and health crazies, and that it's existed for two trillion years before that or whatever. But I'm talking about its newfound widespread acceptance. My two-year-old daughter loves it, and my eighty-three-year-old dad loves it. Neither of them likes baba ghanoush, so I rest my case! This recipe is for every day, and for any occasion.

In a food processor, combine the chickpeas and garlic, and pulse. Add the oil, tahini, lemon juice, cayenne pepper, and salt and pulse a few additional times. If the hummus is too thick, add water 1 tablespoon at a time until the hummus reaches the desired thickness. The hummus will keep in an airtight container in the refrigerator for 3 days.

makes 3 cups

2 (15.5-OUNCE; 440-GRAM) cans chickpeas, rinsed and drained

2 garlic cloves

¼ cup (56 GRAMS) olive oil

¼ cup (57 GRAMS) tahini

2 tablespoons (30 GRAMS) fresh lemon juice

½ teaspoon cayenne pepper

½ teaspoon salt

béchamel sauce

This recipe is to show off. It is for "occasions." It is not the recipe you should turn to daily, or even weekly, if you hope to continue living in the short denim shorts you are wearing right now. But once you've made it, your mind will race with possibilities: Alfredo sauce? Creamed spinach? Lasagna? These are all within reach.

Heat the butter in a wide skillet set over medium heat. Add the onion and cook, stirring, for 2 minutes. Add the garlic and cook, stirring, for 1 more minute. Whisk in the arrowroot and reduce the heat to low. Whisk in the milks, lemon juice, nutritional yeast, and nutmeg, and season with salt and pepper to taste. Cook until the sauce thickens, about 5 more minutes. Remove the pan from the heat and let cool for 5 minutes before serving.

makes 3½ cups

¼ cup (56 GRAMS) Butter (page 133)

2 tablespoons (20 GRAMS) minced onion

2 garlic cloves, minced

3 tablespoons (22 GRAMS) arrowroot

1½ cups (339 GRAMS) rice or almond milk

½ cup (120 GRAMS) coconut milk

1 tablespoon (15 GRAMS) fresh lemon juice

3 tablespoons (27 GRAMS) nutritional yeast

¼ teaspoon ground nutmeg

Salt and freshly ground black pepper

bread reborn

Try as we all might to force-feed both ourselves and those we love, there will be leftovers. Accept it as a blessing, but be prepared to handle those things you can't eat in the first round with care if you want to have a second go at them.

At the bakery, it isn't too often that there are (a) things left over and (b) enough time to experiment with leftovers even if there were any. It is both a godsend (I'm so lucky!) and a sadness (I wanna experiment more!). To be honest, it is partly why I enjoy doing these books so much: Creating recipes lifts me away from my desk duties and puts me back into the test kitchen, where leftovers are invaluable. Often, it is with a single bite of a leftover that you can learn the most. This chapter includes a few of my absolute favorite ways of repurposing baked goods.

For the recipes in this chapter, I used the Sandwich Bread on page 47, mostly for its ability to adapt to and assume the flavors of the other ingredients. By no means is this a rule: If you have a bread on hand and you want to use it in one of these recipes, I support that fully.

bruschetta GARLIC BREAD bread salad STUFFING croutons

bruschetta

Tomato-salad toast: What could possibly be better? There are two keys to making this recipe shine: Find the most beautiful tomatoes in the land, and be very careful not to slice the bread too thin. You're going to want the toasted pieces to hold up under the weight of the sweet, sweet salad.

Preheat the oven to 400°F. Line a rimmed baking sheet with parchment paper and set aside.

In a medium bowl, combine the tomatoes, garlic, 2 tablespoons of the oil, the lemon juice, basil, red pepper flakes, and salt, and season with pepper. Toss well and set aside.

Arrange the slices of bread on the prepared baking sheet. Drizzle the tops with the remaining 2 tablespoons oil.

Bake for 6 minutes, and then rotate the baking sheet 180 degrees. Bake until golden, 3 minutes. Let the toasts cool on the baking sheet for 2 minutes.

To serve, top the toasts with the tomato mixture, drizzle with the liquid from the bowl, and sprinkle with salt and pepper to taste.

serves 6

4 plum tomatoes, chopped

1 garlic clove, minced

¼ cup (56 GRAMS) olive oil

1 tablespoon (15 GRAMS) fresh lemon juice

¼ cup (10 GRAMS) fresh basil leaves, torn

¼ teaspoon crushed red pepper flakes

½ teaspoon salt, plus more for sprinkling

Freshly ground black pepper

½ loaf Sandwich Bread (page 47), cut into 1-inch-thick slices (2½ CUPS; 185 GRAMS)

garlic bread

It is a timeless technique of youth: Nuke your butter in the microwave, pour in *way* too much garlic salt, spread it onto slices of bread so thick it looks like a frosted cake, and shove it under the broiler. Nasty, but in a good way, back then. Nowadays garlic salt tastes to me like it was ground in a metallic tank along with aspirin. So instead of using that, I roast actual garlic and pump it up a little bit with some crushed red pepper flakes.

serves 6

1 head of garlic

2 teaspoons (9 GRAMS) melted unscented coconut oil

1 cup (224 GRAMS) Butter (page 133), softened

1½ teaspoons salt

1 teaspoon crushed red pepper flakes

½ loaf Sandwich Bread (page 47)

Preheat the oven to 275°F.

Trim the tips off the top of the garlic and put it in a small baking dish. Drizzle with the oil. Roast until it becomes soft, 30 minutes. Let it cool for 15 minutes.

Increase the oven temperature to 400°F. Line a baking sheet with parchment paper and set aside.

Squeeze the garlic cloves into a small bowl and discard the husk. Add the butter, salt, and the red pepper flakes and, using a rubber spatula, stir the mixture to form a paste.

Cut the bread lengthwise down the center. Spread the garlic butter generously on the cut sides and put them on the prepared baking sheet, cut side up.

Bake for 8 minutes, and then rotate the baking sheet 180 degrees. Bake until golden brown, 5 minutes. Let the garlic bread cool on the baking sheet for 5 minutes before serving.

bread salad

There is an excellent restaurant in San Francisco named Zuni Café. It opened in 1979, and for the longest time had as its chef the recently deceased genius Judy Rodgers, formerly of Chez Panisse, where I did a stint as a bartender long ago. It was at Zuni, in the late 1990s, that I first learned of bread salad. There Chef Rodgers served it as part of a dinner entrée I could neither afford nor consume. But whenever I'd pop in for a drink at the bar I'd notice waiters carrying large plates piled high with something that to me was just staggering: huge, gorgeous chunks of delicately toasted bread tossed among some greens. This truly was a bread salad. Bread first, and then salad, not as an afterthought, exactly, but as an accent. Much to my dismay I have still never eaten Zuni's version. But this is what I've always imagined it would taste like.

serves 4

- 1 tablespoon (15 GRAMS) red wine vinegar
- 1 garlic clove, minced
- ¼ cup plus 3 tablespoons (98 GRAMS) olive oil
- ½ loaf Sandwich Bread (page 47), cut into 1-inch-thick cubes (2½ CUPS; 185 GRAMS)
- 2 large tomatoes, cut into ½-inch cubes
- 1 cucumber, shaved into ribbons with a vegetable peeler, core discarded
- 1 cup (20 GRAMS) fresh baby arugula or regular arugula
- ½ small red onion, thinly sliced
- 4 basil leaves, torn
- Salt and freshly ground black pepper

In a small bowl, combine the vinegar and garlic. While whisking, slowly drizzle in ¼ cup of the oil. Set aside.

In a medium bowl, toss the bread cubes with the remaining 3 tablespoons oil.

In a wide skillet set over medium heat, toast the bread in batches, cooking until the bottom is golden brown, 2 minutes. Flip the bread and toast the second side 2 more minutes. Return the toasted croutons to the bowl that was used to toss the bread and add the tomatoes, cucumber, arugula, red onion, and basil. Add the vinaigrette and season with salt and pepper to taste. Toss the salad gently until everything is distributed evenly throughout the salad. Serve immediately.

stuffing

You'll be excited to hear that this recipe is simpler than the boxed variety your mother-in-law cherishes, and it tastes about one billion times better. Herbs are absolutely a personal preference, so toss in or remove whatever it is you love or hate. Take note, though, that dried herbs tend to blossom in flavor quite a bit as they cook, so keep it conservative when measuring.

In a dry, wide skillet set over medium heat, toast the walnuts (if using) for 1 minute, stir, and toast until fragrant, 30 more seconds. Transfer the walnuts to a dry paper towel.

Heat the butter in a wide skillet set over medium heat. Add the onion and cook until soft, about 3 minutes. Add the garlic and cook for 30 seconds. Add the bread, sage, walnuts, and nutmeg, season with salt and pepper, and toss well. Let the stuffing cool for 10 minutes before serving.

serves 8

½ cup (64 GRAMS) chopped walnuts (optional)

½ cup (112 GRAMS) Butter (page 133)

½ cup (80 GRAMS) chopped onion

1 teaspoon minced garlic

1 loaf Sandwich Bread (page 47), cut into ½-inch cubes (5 CUPS; 370 GRAMS)

1 tablespoon (1 GRAM) chopped fresh sage leaves

¼ teaspoon ground nutmeg

Salt and freshly ground black pepper

croutons

I eat a salad, in one form or another, for every meal. Each and every time, until this recipe, I coasted sadly past the croutons. Historically it has really sucked. But this is the remedy for all that. I even made them a little spicy.

makes 2½ cups

½ loaf Sandwich Bread (page 47), cut into roughly ½-inch cubes (2½ CUPS; 185 GRAMS)

¼ cup (56 GRAMS) melted Butter (page 133) or melted unscented coconut oil

3 sage leaves, torn

2 teaspoons dried oregano

2 teaspoons salt

Freshly cracked black pepper

Preheat the oven to 400°F. Line a rimmed baking sheet with parchment paper and set aside.

In a medium bowl, toss together the bread, butter, sage, oregano, and salt, and season with pepper. Spread out the seasoned bread on the prepared baking sheet.

Bake, stirring halfway through, until the croutons are golden, about 12 minutes. Let them cool on the baking sheet for 3 minutes before serving. The croutons will keep in an airtight container for 2 days.

sweets: the bonus round

I proved incapable of writing a recipe collection without including a few desserts. Sweets are just who I am. If you are reading this and are happy to find this chapter, please join me in thanking my lovely editor, Rica, and wonderful publisher, Pam, for letting me sneak these recipes into my savory book.

Though to be honest, most of them aren't *that* much of a stretch from the savory premise of this collection. The recipes that follow are largely the result of having loaf upon loaf of leftover bread in the test kitchen. If you've come to know anything about me over the course of these books, it's that I enjoy the color pink and I hate waste in the kitchen: You've worked hard to bring these recipes to life, and they should work equally hard to bring you happiness.

So I took some half-finished croissants, added lots of pantry favorites, and gave to you Sticky Pecan Rolls (page 147). I dosed some shards of a simple bread with cocoa, banana, and dates and now we all can enjoy Banana-Toffee Pudding (page 148). There are also vegan and gluten-free versions of Lorna Doone–like shortbread cookies, cinnamon-sugar twists, and chocolate babka.

sticky
pecan rolls

At the bakery we still do not use nuts of any kind. But at home, I usually have at least a few nut varieties stashed away for eating on the fly, and this is a recipe that reveals the passion for pecans that I'm not able to indulge at the bakery. It's a bit intense, and you should keep it close at hand in the I'm-blowing-my-diet-screw-it file. Close your eyes and go for it.

Melted unscented coconut oil, for brushing the tin

½ cup (112 GRAMS) vegan sugar

2 teaspoons ground cinnamon

1 recipe All-Purpose Puff Pastry Dough (page 110)

½ cup (112 GRAMS) melted Butter (page 133)

1 cup (85 GRAMS) chopped pecans (optional)

¼ cup (88 GRAMS) agave nectar

Preheat the oven to 375°F. Brush 8 cups of a 12-cup muffin tin lightly with oil and set aside.

In a small bowl, whisk together the sugar and cinnamon. Set aside.

Between 2 pieces of parchment paper, roll out the pastry dough into a large 15 by 7-inch rectangle. Remove the parchment paper and cut the dough in half lengthwise. Brush each side with 2½ tablespoons of the melted butter, sprinkle with the cinnamon-sugar, and top with ¾ cup of the pecans (if using), dividing them evenly between the two pieces of dough. Roll each side into a log and cut into 3-inch slices. Put each slice into a muffin cup. Brush with the remaining 3 tablespoons butter, followed by the agave nectar, and then top with the remaining ¼ cup pecans.

Bake for 12 minutes, and then rotate the pan 180 degrees. Bake until golden brown, 10 minutes. Let the pecan rolls cool in the muffin tin for 10 minutes before serving.

banana-toffee pudding

This messy thing has been on my mind for years. I think what prevented me from giving it a try was that it seemed too complicated. Who has the time? It is true that there are more ingredients here than in most other BabyCakes recipes. But really, that is the only intimidating part. Plus in the end you have a glorious thing that everyone else is too intimidated to make for themselves! Upside: You'll be a hero. Downside: You'll be asked to make this for every person's party until the end of time.

You can replace the agave nectar with one cup of vegan sugar or coconut sugar, if you prefer, but be sure to add a few splashes of warm water to the batter so it loosens up and forms something like a pancake batter.

Preheat the oven to 325°F. Brush twelve 3-inch ramekins with oil, arrange them on a baking sheet, and set aside.

In a medium saucepan, bring the 1 cup of water to a boil. Add the dates, reduce the heat, and simmer until all the liquid evaporates, 9 minutes. Remove the pan from the heat and drain off any excess liquid.

In a medium bowl, whisk together the flour, cocoa powder, baking powder, baking soda, xanthan gum, and salt. Add the agave nectar, coconut milk, oil, lukewarm water, and vanilla and whisk until a thick batter forms. Fold in the dates and bananas. Fill each ramekin about two-thirds full with batter.

serves 12

⅓ cup (70 GRAMS) melted unscented coconut oil, plus more for brushing

1 cup (226 GRAMS) water

½ cup (90 GRAMS) pitted dates, roughly chopped

2 cups (280 GRAMS) Bob's Red Mill Gluten-Free All-Purpose Baking Flour

3 tablespoons (18 GRAMS) unsweetened cocoa powder

1½ teaspoons baking powder

1 teaspoon baking soda

¾ teaspoon xanthan gum

1 teaspoon salt

⅔ cup (220 GRAMS) agave nectar

½ cup (120 GRAMS) coconut milk

¼ cup (56 GRAMS) lukewarm water

1 tablespoon (15 GRAMS) pure vanilla extract

1 medium banana, roughly chopped

TOFFEE

¼ cup (56 GRAMS) Butter (page 133)

¼ cup (60 GRAMS) coconut milk

2 tablespoons (28 GRAMS) water

2 teaspoons pure vanilla extract

¾ cup (168 GRAMS) vegan sugar

Pinch of salt

Bake for 10 minutes, and then rotate the baking sheet 180 degrees. Bake until the centers are fully cooked, 8 minutes. Let the puddings cool on the baking sheet for 10 minutes.

Meanwhile, make the toffee: In a small saucepan, combine the butter, coconut milk, water, vanilla, sugar, and salt. Bring to a boil over medium heat, reduce the heat to low, and simmer for 4 minutes. Remove the pan from the heat and let cool for at least 5 minutes to thicken but no more than 15.

Using an oven mitt to hold the ramekins, carefully run a butter knife around the edge of each pudding to loosen it. Turn it out onto a serving plate. Spoon the warm toffee generously over the top. Serve immediately.

cinnamon-sugar pretzels

This is the least sweet dessert I have ever made. It's not unlike Mexico's famous and exceptional churro, though it has a more boring name (nothing beats the word *churro* except for maybe its cousin, *chimichanga*). These pretzels have a few more steps than you are probably accustomed to me providing, but they are not at all difficult. Bake these off by the dozens if you have an outdoor activity to attend or host.

PRETZELS

¾ cup (226 GRAMS) warm water (about 120°F)

6 tablespoons (84 GRAMS) vegan sugar

2¼ teaspoons active dry yeast

2 tablespoons (28 GRAMS) melted unscented coconut oil, plus more for brushing the baking sheet

1¾ cups (245 GRAMS) brown rice flour, or more if needed, plus more for rolling the dough

1 cup (140 GRAMS) Bob's Red Mill Gluten-Free All-Purpose Baking Flour

1 teaspoon xanthan gum

1 teaspoon salt

2 teaspoons pure vanilla extract

3 tablespoons (45 GRAMS) baking soda

CINNAMON-SUGAR

1 cup (224 GRAMS) vegan sugar

2 tablespoons (17 GRAMS) ground cinnamon

Make the pretzels: In a small bowl, combine the warm water, 1 tablespoon of the sugar, and the yeast and let the mixture proof until it bubbles, about 10 minutes. Stir in the coconut oil.

In a medium bowl, whisk together the flours, the remaining 5 tablespoons sugar, the xanthan gum, and salt. Add the yeast mixture and vanilla and, using a rubber spatula, stir until a firm ball of dough forms. If the dough is too wet, add more rice flour 1 tablespoon at a time until it just comes together. Cover the dough with a dish towel and let it sit on the countertop for 1 hour. Wrap the dough in plastic wrap and refrigerate for 2 hours.

Line two baking sheets with parchment paper, brush lightly with oil, and set aside. Make the cinnamon-sugar: Combine the sugar and cinnamon in a small bowl, whisk together, and set aside.

Remove the dough from the refrigerator, unwrap it, and portion out into 14 balls the size of Ping-Pong balls. Using your hands, roll each ball into a rope about 10 inches in length. Twist each rope into a pretzel shape, pressing the ends tightly together so they hold their shape. Put them on the prepared baking sheets.

Preheat the oven to 400°F.

In a large pot set over high heat, bring 3 inches of water to a boil and add the baking soda. Reduce the heat to low. Put 1 pretzel in the water and boil for 45 seconds. Using tongs, turn the pretzel over and cook for 30 more seconds. Transfer the pretzel to a wire rack to drain. Once the pretzel is completely drained, roll in the cinnamon-sugar, then return it to the baking sheet. Repeat this process with the remaining dough, placing the boiled and coated pretzels about 1 inch apart.

Bake for 5 minutes, and then rotate the baking sheets 180 degrees. Bake until browned, 5 minutes. Let the pretzels cool on the baking sheets for 10 minutes before serving.

chocolate babka

I had just finished creating the recipes for this book and was strutting around my local grocery store reveling in the fact that I was done. Then I saw "Chocolate Babka." I put it in my basket. At home I gave a bit to my husband, and a small corner to my daughter. Their eyes lit up the moment they tasted it. The next day at the bakery I made the following version and added the recipe to this book.

Between 2 pieces of parchment paper, roll out the pastry dough into a 14 by 7-inch rectangle about ½ inch thick. Remove the top piece of parchment paper and put the long side of the dough closest to you.

Spread the butter onto the dough, leaving a ½-inch border. Sprinkle the chocolate and sugar on top. Slide a butter knife underneath the dough to loosen it from the paper, and then roll it into a log, pinching the edges to seal. Bring the ends of the log together to form a ring, and pinch to seal. Wrap the pastry ring in plastic wrap, set on a plate, and refrigerate for 1 hour.

Remove the pastry from the refrigerator, carefully unwrap it, and twist the entire ring twice. Place on a piece of parchment paper, grab both ends of the paper, and transfer the dough into a 7 by 4 by 3-inch loaf pan. Let rise at room temperature, lightly covered with a dish towel, for 1 hour.

Preheat the oven to 325°F.

Combine the oil and agave, brush the top of the dough with the mixture, and sprinkle with sugar.

Bake for 25 minutes, and then rotate the pan 180 degrees. Bake until the top is golden, 20 minutes. Let cool in the pan for 20 minutes before serving.

makes one 7 by 4 by 3-inch loaf

½ recipe All-Purpose Puff Pastry Dough (page 110)

4 tablespoons (56 GRAMS) Butter, softened (page 133)

½ cup (112 GRAMS) Enjoy Life semisweet vegan chocolate chips

2 tablespoons (28 GRAMS) vegan sugar, plus more for sprinkling

3 tablespoons (42 GRAMS) melted unscented coconut oil

1 tablespoon (22 GRAMS) agave nectar

shortbread cookies

Even in its simplicity—or perhaps because of it—this cookie is more elegant than others. To me this is the cookie that lady monarchs eat while perched atop large, garish thrones and doling out silent orders with nothing more than a mean twist of the eyebrow. If you absolutely must fuss with it (trust me, bud, you and I are the same), try mixing in chocolate chips or walnuts. Just be sure to chop them up into fairly small pieces.

makes 45

2 cups (280 GRAMS) brown rice flour

1 cup (224 GRAMS) vegan sugar

⅔ cup (80 GRAMS) arrowroot

1 teaspoon xanthan gum

1 teaspoon salt

¾ cup (168 GRAMS) melted unscented coconut oil

2 tablespoons (30 GRAMS) pure vanilla extract

Preheat the oven to 325°F. Line 2 baking sheets with parchment paper and set aside.

In a medium bowl, whisk together the flour, sugar, arrowroot, xanthan gum, and salt. Add the oil and vanilla and, using a rubber spatula, stir until a dough forms. If the dough is too crumbly, add a few tablespoons of water. Wrap the dough in plastic wrap and refrigerate for 1 hour.

Remove the dough from the refrigerator, unwrap it, and put it between 2 pieces of parchment paper. Roll out the dough until it is about ¼ inch thick. Remove the parchment paper and, using a 2-inch cookie cutter, cut the cookies into your desired shape and arrange them on the prepared baking sheets.

Bake until lightly golden brown, about 12 minutes. Let the cookies cool on the baking sheets for 5 minutes before serving.

high-tea cookies

You know that girl who is always sipping a Diet Coke? She could be riding a ski lift or buying fruit for a picnic, leaving the gym at eight a.m. or flagging down a cab at sunrise after leaving the club, and the chick is holding a Diet Coke. That's me, except my Diet Coke is tea (I don't like Diet Coke). I added some teas to the shortbread cookie dough because I like the flavors so much.

Earl Grey: Fold 2 tablespoons (8 grams) dry Earl Grey leaves and 1 teaspoon ground cardamom into the finished dough. After the cookies are baked and cooled, dust lightly with vegan powdered sugar.

Chocolate Chai: Fold 1 tablespoon (6 grams) ground chai and 1 cup (160 grams) vegan chocolate chips into the finished dough.

Chamomile Lavender: Add 2 tablespoons (5 grams) chamomile tea and 1 teaspoon edible lavender to the dough. After the cut cookies are arranged on the baking sheet, sprinkle with vegan sugar for added texture.

lemon sugar cookies

I can sit in a chair staring at a wall eating these cookies and sipping cup after cup of tea for hours on end. They are delicate but satisfying, fruity but not overly sweet. I think of them as comfort food for those of us who are more interested in sweets than we are in lasagna or a bowl of chili. Not that there is anything wrong with either of those things. But I'll take the cookies.

In a food processor, pulse the flours, powdered sugar, lemon zest, salt, and xanthan gum. Add the oil and pulse until the dough becomes sandy. Add the applesauce, vanilla, and lemon extract and pulse until the dough comes completely together. If the dough is too wet, add more rice flour 1 tablespoon at a time. Wrap the dough in plastic wrap, roll it into a 1½-inch-wide log, and refrigerate until firm, about 2 hours.

Preheat the oven to 350°F. Line a baking sheet with parchment paper and set aside.

Spread the granulated sugar across a piece of parchment paper. Remove the log from the refrigerator, unwrap it, and roll it through the sugar until it is fully coated. Slice the log into ¼-inch-thick slices and arrange the slices on a baking sheet about 1 inch apart.

Bake for 7 minutes, and then rotate the baking sheet 180 degrees. Bake until the cookies are golden, 5 minutes. Let the cookies cool on the baking sheet for 5 minutes before serving.

makes 36

- 1½ cups (210 GRAMS) Bob's Red Mill Gluten-Free All-Purpose Baking Flour
- ½ cup (70 GRAMS) brown rice flour, plus more if needed
- 1 cup (100 GRAMS) vegan powdered sugar
- 1 tablespoon (30 GRAMS) grated lemon zest
- 1½ teaspoons salt
- 1 teaspoon xanthan gum
- ¾ cup (168 GRAMS) melted unscented coconut oil
- ⅓ cup (80 GRAMS) unsweetened applesauce
- 2 tablespoons (30 GRAMS) pure vanilla extract
- 1 teaspoon lemon extract
- ½ cup (112 GRAMS) vegan granulated sugar, for rolling

acknowledgments

This page should be the easiest, most enjoyable one to write. In truth, I find it the most difficult by far. It is impossible to fully capture and explain how important these people are to me.

MY DEEPEST LOVE, AFFECTION, AND THANKS TO . . .

My darling daughter, Halsey Valentine. I cannot in this space express all you are to me. *Everything* is too small a word.

My sweetly patient and otherwise completely magnificent and gorgeous agent, Kim Witherspoon, with the lovely Allison Hunter, at Inkwell. I am so grateful for you both. You make it all seem so much easier than I know it is.

Pam Krauss, Rica Allannic, and Jane Treuhaft at Clarkson Potter. I am so thankful to you for giving me room to do my thing, but not so much that I veered off course into a lonely and embarrassing ditch. All authors should be so lucky. Thank you to the whole Clarkson Potter team: Ashley Tucker, Patricia Shaw, Heather Williamson, Carly Gorga, Sean Boyles, Doris Cooper, and Aaron Wehner.

My business partner, friend, and collaborator, Sabrina Wells. You are the reason we're able to build this thing of ours. Thank you for giving me the gift of trust and affording me the time away to do all those business things you hate doing anyway! Also, thank you for being so psychotic about people keeping their areas clean.

My beautiful sister, Elizabeth Christie. Thank you for handling with ease and grace the three billion bits of bakery business I've slammed into your job description. You are irreplaceable.

Eddie, Kristi, and the rest of the bakers at BabyCakes who patiently tested my recipes to work out the kinks. Although some early recipes bordered on comical, you kept a straight face and gave me honest feedback. I can't hug you enough!

My beloved Bakery Crew, including but not limited to our hard-working Disney World ambassador Emily Woesthoff and our general managers Gretchen Capitan of Los Angeles and Amy Lachenauer of New York. You are the heartbeat of the bakery and I can't live without you. Thank you for being perfect.

The wondrously talented photographers Clarke Tolton and Davide Luciano, the whip-smart food stylist Claudia Ficca, and the eagle-eyed prop stylist Maeve Sheridan. Thank you for your active and inspired creativity in this collaboration. I'm so love-struck by your interpretation of these recipes I could cry.

Many thanks to Sofia Reino for recipe testing and insights.

My sisters, brothers, and mother. With everything I do, I feel your presence and encouragement surrounding me. Thank you for giving me your love and support with no bounds.

To my late father, Frank McKenna. Thanks for instilling a deep respect for desserts in me and always encouraging me to order the entire dessert menu saying, "You're worth it!" I miss you terribly.

I'd be a very tired-looking shell of a girl without my dream of a beauty department, so thank you Dina Gregg and Sera Sloane for polishing me up the way I like!

Our loving customers. Truly, you feed me and my bakery as much as we feed you. Thank you for never wavering in your support and for showing your love, always.

My husband, Chris Cechin-De la Rosa. You take such sweet and patient care of me. We did it. Again. I love you.

index